Won by Love

Won by Love

NORMA MCCORVEY,
JANE ROE OF *ROE V. WADE,*
SPEAKS OUT FOR THE UNBORN AS SHE
SHARES HER NEW CONVICTION FOR LIFE

NORMA MCCORVEY
WITH GARY THOMAS

JD A JAN DENNIS BOOK

THOMAS NELSON PUBLISHERS
Nashville

Published in Nashville, Tennessee, by Thomas Nelson, Inc., Publishers.

Library of Congress Cataloging-in-Publication Data

McCorvey, Norma, 1947–
Won by love : Norma McCorvey, Jane Roe of Roe v. Wade, speaks out against abortion as she shares her new conviction for life / Norma McCorvey; with Gary Thomas.
p. cm.
Includes bibliographical references.
ISBN 0-7852-8654-3 (hardcover)
1. McCorvey, Norma, 1947– . 2. Roe, Jane, 1947– . 3. Pro-life movement. 4. Christian biography—United States.
I. Thomas, Gary (Gary Lee) II. Title.
BR1725.M3564A3 1998
261.8'3667'092—dc21
[B] 97-29645
CIP

Printed in the United States of America

1 2 3 4 5 6 BVG 02 01 00 99 98 97

This book is dedicated to all the children
who have been torn apart by abortion—
I'm sorry you are no longer here,
but now you are in heaven
with our Father—
And to all the women who through abortion
have had their lives changed—
Amazing Grace can heal your heart,
and you, too, can be won
by love.

CONTENTS

ACKNOWLEDGMENTS

I'd like to prayerfully thank:

The Lord Jesus Christ for always being there for me and for bringing me home to Him.

Emily and Chelsey Mackey for being Emily and Chelsey Mackey! (Especially Emily for her faith in God's willingness to answer prayer and Miss Chelsey for her wonderful child's logic.)

My parents in Christ, Ron and Ronda Mackey (a.k.a. The Street Woman) for believing in me and for their prayers, unconditional love, and lots of Mexican food.

A big Texas thank you goes to Gary Thomas (and the Thomas family), who's spiritual armor never got rusty and who relied on the Holy Spirit throughout this project. He was a driving force behind my ministry to speak out against the enemy.

A heartfelt thanks to Connie Gonzales for sharing her story once again, this time as my sister in Christ.

I thank Pastor Morris Sheats at my home church, Hillcrest, and his assistant, Miss Patty, for always encouraging me when times got rough.

I thank Rev. Philip "Flip" Benham for making me study the Word and for being my spiritual guide for my first two years in Christ and the O.R. family—Miss Annie, Jessie Ann, Mr. Rene, and Brother Mark—who always stood between me and the devil even if that took them into the driveways of the killing places.

I thank Randall Terry—his tireless efforts on behalf of the unborn will not go unrecognized. I thank you especially for forgiving me when I blew that whistle in your face before I knew Christ!

A hearty thank you to Belinda Bass for always knowing who to direct me to at Thomas Nelson, and to Todd Ross, my editor-at-large, for understanding what a relatively new Christian goes through when writing a Christian book.

To Janet Thoma, whose support, encouragement, and oversight made this book possible. Her ministry to Christian authors—past, present, and, I hope, long into the future—has been phenomenal. She's one of the toughest yet, in her own way, gentlest Christian professionals I've ever met—an inspired mix, to be sure.

And finally, to all the Christians who have ever prayed for me throughout these years, both before I became a Christian and after—your prayers were heard and answered, and I thank you for uttering them, with all my heart.

In His Service,
Norma McCorvey

CHAPTER 1

My Neighbor, the Terrorist

If I had known March 31, 1995, was going to be such a bad day, I probably would have checked out of life right then and there. But I was oblivious to all that lay ahead as I answered my phone and heard the news that exploded my comfortable world.

"You'll never guess who's moving in next door," I heard a woman from the abortion clinic say.

"John Travolta," I offered.

"No."

"Humphrey Bogart?"

"No."

"Then who?" I was not in a mood to play games.

"Try Operation Rescue."

I immediately fumbled around and lit up a second cigarette, even though I already had one burning. They don't make nicotine strong enough for situations like this one.

"You've got to be kidding, of course," I said, feigning laughter. "This is a joke, right?"

"I'm afraid not. You ought to come down and see for yourself."

The clinic worker's tone overcame my doubts, and I hung up the phone in shock. For me, Norma McCorvey, also known as Jane Roe of the infamous *Roe v. Wade* abortion decision, to have Operation Rescue for a next-door neighbor was like having the Hatfields move in next door to the McCoys. My most bitter enemies and I would be sharing a common wall. I could feel a headache coming on.

For forty-some years I had played it tough. I was Jane Roe, I could handle anything. But the truth is, I felt so weak that I knew I needed help, yet there was no spiritual strength for me to draw upon. My hands were shaking too much to consult the Ouija board, so I considered my two standbys: drugs and constant activity.

Since the nicotine wasn't working, I called the press. Channel 4 in Dallas was always one of my favorites. As an abortion advocate, my views were consistently well represented on that network, and I knew I would get a sympathetic (if not an overtly biased) hearing. I got hold of a producer and announced, "Have I got a story for you guys."

"What is it, Norma?" he asked.

"Seems like Operation Rescue is moving next door to the abortion clinic where I work."

"You're kidding. O.R. is moving next door to Jane Roe's abortion clinic?"

"That's right."

"This is too much!"

"Well, let me get down there and see what's going on. I'll fill you in."

The circus had begun.

A Mad Dash

It took me seven minutes to complete what was normally a fifteen-minute trip. The last thing I could do was sit still, so I drove as fast as I could, inhaling on my cigarettes with a greedy passion. I couldn't get the nicotine into my system fast enough.

On the drive over, I became convinced that somebody must be playing a cruel joke on me. The landlord had promised that our abortion clinic could have the space into which O.R. was reputed to be moving. We were planning to expand. We even had a key to the front door! How in the world could the landlord turn around and rent the space to O.R.?

It was impossible.

I pulled off the LBJ Highway and onto Markville Drive, the side street housing our clinic in the Lake Highlands area of north Dallas. A Choice for Women was located in an aging one-story office building that is U-shaped with a huge parking lot in the center. The abortion clinic was at the bottom of the U, set back about a hundred yards from any public walkway. That was not by accident. We had to have sufficient private property so that the "O.R. Terrorists" (as we thought of them) could not legally set up camp outside our front door or even demonstrate in a place where they could reach our clients.

Which reminded me: *If we thought we had to protect ourselves from O.R. with a distant sidewalk, how in the world could we survive if we shared a common wall?*

As I pulled into the parking lot, I breathed a sigh of relief. There wasn't an O.R. person to be found. The call *must* have been a joke. Somebody was trying to catch me on April Fools' Day, one day early. Well, I would have some explaining to do to Channel 4, but that was better than having to live next door to Flip Benham (in private, we liked to call him Flip Venom), O.R.'s fiery director.

I walked into the clinic, finally feeling calm enough to put out my cigarette, and said, "All right, who came in with the hangover? What's all this about O.R. moving in next door?"

My lifelong friend, Connie Gonzales—the person whom I trusted most in this world—walked up to me and said, "Norma, it's true."

Connie would not lie. Not about this. She had been there the night I was targeted for "execution" by antichoice terrorists. Violence against abortion clinic doctors and personnel had been increasing for the past several years, making me a prime target, so Connie knew this was nothing to joke about.

Connie saw my stunned expression. "If you don't believe me," she said, "look outside now."

I turned around and my mouth dropped open as I saw Flip Venom and his two cohorts driving up in a large Ryder truck.

"I need another cigarette," I said.

"You just finished one," someone said.

"Then give me two."

The Headache Next Door

Watching O.R. move in next door was like going to a horror movie only to find out when you returned home that Freddy Krueger had bought the house across the street. I saw anti-choicers (or antis for short) as vicious, mean-spirited, fire-breathing, sanctimonious, self-righteous, bigoted hypocrites who wanted nothing more than to see Jane Roe, the woman responsible for legalized abortion, dead.

In fact, some pro-lifers, who didn't know I was Jane Roe at the time, told me as much to my face. "I'd like to get hold of that Jane Roe and kill her myself," one of them had told me.

From the look on her face, I believed her (and kept my identity to myself!).

I walked outside the clinic and dropped into a catatonic stare as Flip parked his rental truck and started waving at me. The last time I had seen Flip was when he crowded into a book signing and shouted at me that I should be ashamed of myself for causing the deaths of thirty-five million children. This time, he smiled, jumped out of his truck, and yelled, "Hellooo, Miss Norma!"

My first instinct was to call the police. Flip couldn't be on our property; it was trespassing. Unless—unless he really was a legal tenant!

Well, I don't know who called them (it wasn't me), but the police did show up rather quickly. The officers were visibly upset and impatient and immediately informed Flip that he was under arrest. He had been arrested on this site several times before, and this time, as far as they were concerned, was no different.

I smiled. *That problem's solved,* I thought, my headache already beginning to go away. We could always count on the Dallas police.

"You can't arrest me," Flip protested. "I'm leasing the office suite right next door. I have every right to use this parking lot."

"Don't play games with us," the officer growled.

"I'm telling you, this is my office, I'm gonna stay here, and you're not going to arrest anybody."

The police officers knew Flip could be bold and even brash, but he wasn't stupid. They checked out his story and found out it was true, so Flip was free to roam.

The police officers looked over at me and shrugged their shoulders. There was nothing they could do.

My headache came rushing back.

"Want to Join Us?"

A little later in the day, Flip called out, "Hey, Miss Norma! We're about to have a pizza. Want to join us?"

"I can't eat cheese," I said. "I'm lactose intolerant."

Pizza, my eye! Who did he think he was, driving up to my clinic and inviting me to lunch? As if I'd accept anything from him without having it tested by a lab first!

I went back into the clinic and saw Lynn, a worker in our abortion clinic, kicking the wall.

"What in the world are you doing, Lynn? Have you lost your mind?" I asked.

"If we make enough noise, maybe they'll go away."

"Look," I shouted, losing my temper. "I've got enough on my hands trying to deal with the crazy people moving in. If you all go crazy on me, I might just lose my own mind, too, so knock it off! It's gonna take a lot more than a bit of noise to make these people go away."

The abortion doctor, "Arnie," ran up the hall. "Norma, what do we do?"

"How should I know, Arnie?" I asked. "You think they make instruction manuals for this?"

One of the reasons Arnie was so scared was that, quite recently, a well-known abortion clinic in the Dallas area—the A to Z Clinic—had been subjected to O.R. protests and had subsequently closed down. O.R. called a press conference, claiming credit, but I knew the real story because I had worked there while I was also working at A Choice for Women. The truth is, the A to Z Clinic was a sorry mess.

A Sorry Mess

I started working at the A to Z Clinic in January 1995, and it was a health disaster waiting to happen. If the owner had not closed it down, eventually even the government would have been forced to do it. Light fixtures hung out of the ceiling; falling plaster dusted everyone who walked by. Next door to the clinic was an abandoned warehouse full of boxes and newspapers, so we fought an ongoing, and losing, battle with the rat population that resided there. Every morning we found rat droppings all over the clinic. Sinks were backed up—in a reputed medical clinic, no less—and blood splatters stained the walls.

The "Parts Room," where we kept the aborted babies, was particularly heinous. No one liked to be in there to do their business, much less to clean the place, and since no patients were allowed back there, it was pretty much left to ruin. If a baby didn't make it into a bucket, that was too bad; it was left to lay there. Other babies were stacked like cordwood once every body part had been accounted for (after abortions, doctors have to account for major body parts—arms, legs, torso, and head—to make sure nothing is left inside the mother).

The room smelled awful. We used Pine-Sol because of its strong antiseptic smell, but within hours the cleaning mixture was overpowered by the smell of medical waste and rot—which explains why the rats were so eager to visit us every night.

The floor of the clinic invited contamination. It was covered by an old, gold-and-brown shag rug. At least I think it was gold and brown—no one really knew for sure, since the rug had not been cleaned for a long time.

When the out-of-town owner realized he had a tremendous financial liability just waiting to happen, he shut the clinic doors. He really didn't have any choice.

O.R. had taken credit for the closure, saying that their protests had resulted in the owner's decision. At the time, I never gave any thought to how God might sovereignly work in response to prayer, so I thought O.R. was nothing but a bunch of grandstanding liars.

Now Arnie was afraid; I could see it in his face. And, with O.R. moving next door, he had reason to be.

Arnie is a small man of foreign descent. It's a closely guarded fact that a disproportionate number of abortion doctors are actually from other countries—foreigners who perceive that our lax abortion laws create a tremendous moneymaking opportunity. Because of the politics surrounding abortion and the unparalleled success of the abortion lobby, veterinary clinics have stricter regulations than abortion clinics.

Foreign-born abortionists don't have to worry about acquiring bedside manners. They don't even have to talk to the patients if they don't want to, so it's a practice ready-made for someone who simply wants to show up, do his dirty work, and go home with a fistful of cash.

Arnie is five feet three inches tall, with a good paunch. He always goes barefoot, even when he's operating. He has green eyes and carefully cropped hair, and he speaks with a strong accent.

Whenever I would walk back into the clinic during my forays with O.R.'s moving-in crew, Arnie would ask me, "Norma, what is going on now?"

"They're still moving in, Doctor."

"This is not good, Norma, this is not good. What are we going to do?"

The thing that worried Arnie most was that Flip Benham, the man who had taken on and defeated A to Z, was now next door to *his* clinic, threatening his livelihood and his six-figure income.

Flipper

The man of Arnie's nightmares, Flip Benham, reminds me of a beach guy. Whereas I could have picked up Arnie with one hand, I'd need a truck to move Flip, who is built like a stocky surfer and is over six feet tall. He has a thick head of hair, even in his late forties.

Flip has a Bat Masterson kind of arrogance and walks with the swagger of a riverboat gambler. But even back then, when he was my worst enemy, I could see a gentleness to his toughness, and something drew me to him.

Since I had already said I couldn't eat a pizza, when I went back outside Flip asked if I wanted a sandwich. "Oh no, don't bother," I said. "I don't think I could eat today at all. I'll just drink my lunch and dinner."

I didn't know this at the time, but Flip had been a saloon-owning alcoholic. I intentionally tried to shock him by talking about drinking my meals, but Flip was intimately familiar with an alcoholic's favorite method of "medicating" stress.

The press was eating this up. It was a circus outside, with flashbulbs popping and video cameras rolling and interviews taking place on a constant basis. One reporter would talk to Flip, then come over and get my reaction; this type of thing went on all afternoon, until I began to lose what little patience I had.

I kept looking at Flip, thinking, *Why here? There are ten thousand different offices in Dallas, Texas; why did you have to move next door to* my *clinic?* We were standing side by side, less than ten feet apart, when Flip started egging me on.

"Are you still killing babies, Miss Norma?" Flip asked me.

"Oh come on, Flip," I said. "Lighten up. What you need is to go to a good Beach Boys concert."

"Miss Norma," Flip said, completely taking me by surprise, "I haven't been to a Beach Boys concert since 1976."

All at once—and I mean that; it was a sudden realization—Flip became more human to me. Before, I had thought of him as a man who did nothing but yell at abortion clinics and read his Bible. In fact, I even pictured him sleeping with his hands crossed over his chest, Dracula-style, with a big Bible tucked under one arm. The thought that he was a real person—a guy who had once gone to a Beach Boys concert—never occurred to me. Now that it had, I saw him in a new light.

This sudden realization did not comfort me, however. On the contrary, it made me more nervous. The real person scared me even more than the imagined terrorist. When he had screamed at me, he looked like a mountain rolling my way. *That man is big,* I thought. *That man could hurt me. I need to get away.*

But now I thought he might be fun to get to know. And that thought really scared me. I tried to pierce through this by teasing him. "Come on, Flip, I didn't know you were ever a sinner."

"Miss Norma," Flip said, "I'm a great big sinner saved by a great big God." And he smiled.

Of all the things I expected Flip to say, this wasn't one of them. Flip, a sinner? Flip, a human being?

Again, I was shaken. I wanted to think of Flip as the man I had watched on the television screen as he laid his body in front of an abortion clinic in Wichita. The whole thing seemed unreal to me. I kept asking myself, *What would drive so many people to give up four to six weeks of their lives to travel to Wichita, knowing that they would be thrown into jail?* I mean, I gave up a lot of my time to push for legal abortion, but these people were willing to *go to jail* to stop it. I never met a pro-choice group with that kind of commitment.

I remembered watching another rescue and seeing the police roughly drag rescuers away from the clinic doors. Some of them had even chained themselves to stair railings; they were willing to do whatever it took to keep the clinics closed.

In my mind, that bordered on fanaticism. These weren't real people, not like my friends and I were real. These antichoicers were otherworldly; they didn't feel the same things I felt.

And yet now Flip was telling me that he was a sinner. A chill worked its way up to my heart. What if the same thing that happened to Flip happened to me?

Nah. Couldn't happen. Not to Norma McCorvey. Not to Jane Roe. God wouldn't have her.

Still, there was something that bothered me greatly. Flip had a certain undeniable charisma. Something inside me made me want to tell him my whole life story. *Maybe then he would understand*, I thought. *Maybe then he wouldn't hate me so much.*

It was a strange feeling, wanting my archenemy to hear my life story, so I coped with it the way I always did. I left the clinic, went to a restaurant, and began lushing beer, not quite finishing a six-pack.

A couple of hours later, I called Connie. "Can you pick me up?" I asked. "I'm not in any shape to drive."

Some years ago, Connie and I had been lovers, but our relationship had been completely platonic since 1992, though we still shared a home. To be honest, I had grown weary of the homosexual lifestyle. Connie and I had been friends before we ever became lovers, and now that I was "grown up" and no longer worried about getting pregnant by another man, I simply had no desire to continue a sexual relationship.

When Connie drove up, she was still wearing her scrubs from work. Connie served as the clinic supervisor and office manager. Technically, that made her my boss. She is dark complexioned, of Spanish and Italian descent, and her naturally black hair was just beginning to frost into white as she approached her sixty-fifth birthday.

The day's events had taken their toll on Connie as much as they had on me. She looked every bit her age that night. I quietly climbed into the truck, and then, after a silent drive, stumbled into the house. I went straight for the shower, letting the hot water burn my skin. When the water started to grow cold, I stepped out of the shower, dressed, and fell into bed, crying myself to sleep.

I just didn't want to believe that this day had actually happened.

But it had. It really had.

CHAPTER

2 Shots in the Night

Six years earlier, almost to the day, I was lying on the couch watching television. It was getting late and I thought, *Maybe I should just sleep here.* I felt myself start to doze, but then, for some reason, decided to get up and go to bed.

That decision saved my life.

Several hours later, I was catapulted from my sleep with the sound of a shotgun discharge tearing into my front door.

Rat-tat-tat-tat-tat. I heard the pellets slapping against the storm door, tearing it to pieces.

"Connie!" I screamed, yelling at her to get up. I instinctively turned the corner out of my bedroom and entered the hallway leading into the living room. It was a stupid thing to do, but thinking through how you should respond to having your house shot up is not exactly standard procedure.

As soon as I rounded the corner, another blast demolished our front window and scattered shot pell-mell throughout the living room. Several tore into the couch where I had been lying just a few hours before; others scattered themselves along our dining room wall.

A single pellet whizzed by my right ear, jamming my sense of hearing and making me feel like I must have been hit. It hurt, I was frightened, and I screamed, wondering if I was going to die.

Connie grabbed me around the waist and pulled me to the ground, then rolled over on top of me, shielding my body from the next shot. We heard a truck jam its gears, turn around, and speed down the street once again. The assailants sent another blast into our car, then took off in a black pickup with a gun rack in the back—as effective a disguise as you could hope for in Dallas, Texas. It would take the police years to search for every black truck in the city.

I flinched as the last blast hit the metal of our car, parked outside in the driveway. My nerves were already shot. Though the entire attack was over in seconds, it felt as if it had lasted forever.

"Somebody Wants to Kill Me!"

We were afraid to get up for several minutes, so we just lay there, our chests heaving as if we had run a mile-long race. The silence that followed was eerie. Dogs started barking, first one, and then several, but beyond that there was a disbelieving hush.

When I opened my eyes, stars danced in front of me. My head felt like I had been hit with a baseball bat. I checked for blood, but couldn't find any, though my hearing was all stuffed up.

"Oh, no!" Connie moaned. "Look at the dining room wall."

It was completely shot up.

I finally got to my feet and called 911, and the police arrived within minutes. The local officer who responded started asking the usual questions: Had we broken up with anyone? Did we owe anyone money? Were we dealing drugs?

It was hard to be patient. I knew exactly what was going on. It was April 4, 1989, the day before Connie and I were scheduled to fly to Washington, D.C., to participate in the biggest rally ever organized in support of legalized abortion. Violence against abortion providers was on the rise, and it only made sense that I would be at the top of the opposition's hit list.

I let Connie handle the police officers and picked up the phone, dialing information.

"Get me the number for the FBI," I said.

My hands were shaking so much, it was almost impossible to write down the number as the operator gave it, but I somehow managed to do it. When I dialed the number, I was surprised that someone answered so early in the morning.

"This is Norma McCorvey," I said, "Jane Roe of *Roe v. Wade*. Somebody just shot up our house. I think they may have been trying to kill me."

And then, I broke. I don't know if it was the bad hearing I fought in one ear, the bullet-marked dining room wall, the stars dancing before my eyes, or the inane questioning by the local police officer in the background, but something made me snap. I became hysterical, wailing and collapsing onto the floor. I was overwhelmed by the fact that somebody hated me enough to want to kill me.

Connie came over to me, picked up the phone, and completed the call. The FBI arrived almost immediately. They swarmed the house, covering and inspecting every inch. I was standing off to the side, still not quite believing what was going on, when one of the FBI officers introduced himself and handed me his card.

"My wife works for Planned Parenthood," he said.

"Does that make you pro-choice?" I asked.

"Yes."

I breathed a sigh of relief. I needed the security of a sympathetic believer.

"We're making arrangements to get you out of the neighborhood as soon as possible," he assured me.

It didn't take long for the media to arrive. At this point, relatively few people knew me as Jane Roe, but this sort of blew my cover, at least locally. Some have accused me of wanting the attention, but let me ask you how you'd feel if you had just learned that people wanted to kill you, and that the media was now broadcasting pictures of your house all over the world?

This was attention I could do without.

I stood there in disbelief. Why would somebody want to kill me over a political issue? That's all abortion was to me—a political issue. I didn't understand how my work could inspire such violence. After all, I had never even had an abortion.

What was their problem?

A Reluctant Icon

Part of my confusion over why somebody would want to kill me—and I should mention that it's never been proved that the people who shot up my house had any connection with a pro-life group—came from my ambivalence about the issue. Talking about my ambivalence concerning abortion might shock some people, but it's true. Even though I allowed my name to go on the affidavit that resulted in the dismantling of every state's laws restricting abortion, I was never very comfortable with the act of abortion itself.

That made for some difficult encounters. I remember one rally in particular, where a young woman approached me. She was very cute with long, straight hair, great big green eyes, and fair skin.

"So, you're Jane Roe?" she said.

"That's right."

"Wow. Can I touch you?"

"Where?" I said immediately. I was always on my guard!

"I just think it's, like, cool—what you've done; how you've made it possible for me to get my abortions."

"Abor*tions*?" I said, stressing the plural. "How many have you had?"

"I don't know." The girl shrugged. "Five or six, I guess."

I cringed. The girl noticed it, but my act was involuntary. I wasn't trying to be cruel, but even back then I knew getting an abortion was not like getting a haircut.

"How come you had that many?" I asked. "Didn't you learn anything after the first time?"

I could understand a woman making one mistake. I could even understand a woman making the same mistake twice. But half a dozen times? I'm sorry. I didn't have any patience for that.

I had to get away from her. I couldn't stand there and talk to her anymore.

I left the rally early, the girl's words, "I don't know, five or six, I guess" ringing in my ears, haunting me, and went directly to a bar, where I downed a couple of shots of straight tequila. I waited for the alcohol to take effect before I went back to my room to chase it down with five or six beers.

On other occasions, I drowned out the reality of what I had done by turning to marijuana—not that I needed much of an excuse to get high. Sometimes I would turn the television on as loud as I thought I could get away with so that I could cry without anyone knowing it.

I was deathly afraid of anyone hearing me cry. I was supposed to be Jane Roe, superhero of the abortion movement. I wasn't supposed to be weak. I wasn't supposed to have deep regrets when women thanked me for giving them the right to abort five or six babies.

I wasn't supposed to have feelings, but I did. And they hurt.

Given the volatile situation surrounding the abortion debate, the FBI decided after the shooting that I needed to be removed from my house immediately. Agents took me out the back door, helped me over a fence, and took me to the local Holiday Inn. It was very cloak-and-dagger. As we drove down my street, I shook my head when I saw armed guards posted at the front door of my shot-up house. Seeing the house like that reminded me of a Nazi movie I had watched a few weeks before.

CHAPTER 3

"Did You Say You're Jane Roe?"

Two days later, Connie and I flew into Washington, D.C., under the names Smith and Jones (how's that for creativity?). Though somebody in the pro-life movement was apparently paying me too much attention, in Washington I received exactly the opposite. In fact, I was never even formally invited to the April 9 march. Not a single person from the organizing committee came to greet me at the airport. I knew that many other events were going on around the march, but I wasn't invited to a single one.

Even so, I had prepared a little speech, just in case. I still couldn't believe that Jane Roe would not be asked to say *something,* even if she was blue-collar and didn't quite fit in with the Ivy League–educated feminists who ran the abortion movement. My pedigree, apparently, was an embarrassment to the Vassar-degreed lawyers. My grandmother had made a living as a prostitute and then, as she grew older, a fortune-teller. My mother was an alcoholic Roman Catholic, my father a Jehovah's Witness and television repairman. I'm part Cajun and Cherokee Indian with a ninth-grade education. When people talk about "pumps," I assume they're referring to gasoline, not shoes.

With this background, it's not so surprising that I had a difficult time fitting in with women who wore business suits and carried briefcases. Most of my friends were drug pushers or poor people or carnival workers. I met my closest friend, Connie, when she caught me shoplifting at her store.

Yet in spite of this background—or maybe because of it—I ended up being the lead plaintiff in the case that brought legalized abortion to the United States. Though I had recently begun letting people know that I was Jane Roe, there had never been a national "coming out." NBC had run a movie of my life, but they changed my name to protect my privacy.

In 1989 few recognized me or knew Jane Roe by the name Norma McCorvey. But the march organizers knew. Certainly Sarah Weddington, the lawyer who represented me in the case, knew. Yet most of the leaders didn't really care. That's how I could travel to the march and still be anonymous.

Jane Roe Says No

The morning of the march, I joined in with the Texas contingency, hanging out with about twenty people from the Dallas area. My friends were growing increasingly frustrated as it looked ever more certain that I'd be shut out of the rally completely. Earlier in the month, we had discussed it. A reporter from *People* magazine happened to be with several of us that night, and when the topic of the march came up, she kept saying, "I can't believe they don't want you to speak."

I shrugged my shoulders. "I'm not a very good speaker, anyway."

Sarah, one of my friends, promised, "I'm gonna get you on that stage."

"Don't bother," I told her.

Finally, in the middle of the march, another of my friends couldn't take it anymore, and she began shouting, "Jane Roe, she says no! Jane Roe, she says no! Jane Roe, she says no!"

Soon, the entire march seemed to be saying it in unison. Nobody knew what Jane Roe was saying "no" to (least of all, Jane Roe!), but I felt funny hearing my pseudonym chanted by people who had no idea I was marching right next to them.

I wore a blue sweatshirt that had been given to me by the NBC producer who had worked on the television movie. It had the words *Supreme Court, Roe v. Wade* on it, and a woman walked up and asked me, "Where did you get that shirt? I like it."

"A woman who works for NBC designed it for me," I said.

"Oh, yeah?" she asked. "Well, who are you?"

"I'm Jane Roe."

"Yeah, right," she muttered. You could see what she was thinking: *If you're really Jane Roe, what are you doing marching in the back?*

Once the march was over, we gathered in front of the Capitol. My friend Sarah got up and left, returning about ten minutes later. She had a mischievous look on her face.

"What are you up to, Sarah?" I asked.

"Oh, about five six."

The next thing I knew, a lady with an official-looking badge came down and spotted Sarah. Sarah pointed to me and then introduced us. "I just had to see if you were really here," the woman said.

"I are here," I replied.

"I'll let the others know," she said.

"Whatever."

It was becoming embarrassing.

About ten minutes later the official came back and motioned for Sarah and me to join her behind the stage. The place was packed and looked like an Academy Awards ceremony with all the stars walking around. My friend Sarah immediately started mingling, but I stayed off to one side. I saw an attractive blond woman wearing diamond-studded cowboy boots and decided to try my hand at being friendly. "Girlfriend, aren't you afraid you're gonna get them things dirty?"

She looked at me and I realized I was talking to Morgan Fairchild, the actress. "Well that's okay," she said. "I had them made especially for this occasion."

I began to understand why I didn't fit in. Morgan Fairchild's boots, "made especially for this occasion," cost more than my entire wardrobe put together.

Lily Tomlin walked by. I saw Molly Yard from NOW (the National Organization for Women), and then Ali McGraw. Finally, I got the nerve to approach Ali and said, "Are you really who I think you are?"

"Well that depends. Who do you think I am?"

"Ali McGraw."

"Yes, I'm her."

"Wow," I said.

In spite of the celebrity sightings, I grew increasingly miserable. I knew I didn't fit in. Even my clothes were out of place. Everyone had been encouraged to wear white because groups wearing white look bigger than groups wearing dark colors. I don't know why, but I wore a blue shirt and white pants.

Gloria

As time passed, I became sick to my stomach and needed to use a bathroom, but I didn't have a clue about where I might find one. I was thirsty, desperately craved a cigarette, and couldn't recall a time when I had felt more uncomfortable.

I must have looked quite a sight, because a dark-haired woman came charging up to me with concern all over her face and said, "Are you okay?"

"No, I'm not. I'm thirsty and I need to go to the bathroom."

"My name's Gloria Allred." She held out her hand. I didn't have a clue about who Gloria Allred was, but I knew she must be somebody important if she got to stand behind the stage.

"If you need to go to the bathroom, I can fix that," she said, then motioned for me to follow.

Gloria led me inside the Capitol and began telling me about who she was. I learned that she was a prominent civil rights attorney from Los Angeles who had represented Patty Hearst (several years later, she would represent one of the victims' families through the early days of the O. J. Simpson fiasco).

Gloria began quizzing me about why I was at the march and how I had ended up behind the stage. We were in the bathroom, and just before she entered a stall I explained, "My name's Norma McCorvey, but a lot of people know me as Jane Roe."

"That's nice," she said, taking one step forward. Suddenly she darted back out of the stall. "Did you say your name was *Jane Roe*?"

"Yeah, of *Roe v. Wade*."

"Why aren't you up onstage with the other VIPs?"

"They don't like me too much."

Gloria began testing me to see if I really was Jane Roe. "Wasn't it Linda Coffee who argued the case before the Supreme Court?" she asked, knowing full well it wasn't.

"No, it was Sarah Weddington."

After a few questions such as this, Gloria finally believed me, then stayed with me the rest of the day, showing me how much difference the concern of one person can make. She tried to arrange a meeting between me and Sarah Weddington, but when Gloria approached her, Sarah said, "Not now, I'm busy."

Gloria came back and tried to ease me away from the hurt. "You know, that girl really is busy," she said, but both she and I knew Sarah's refusal to talk to me had more behind it than that. Sarah had all the time in the world for me before I signed up as her plaintiff; but once she had my signature, I was a blue-collar, rough-talking embarrassment.

Gloria was the first person to really understand how I felt about being ignored, so she pointed out some people from the press area and said, "Look, I know these guys. I think you should give a little interview."

"Oh, no, I don't think so. That's not why I came here."

But Gloria grabbed my elbow and said, "Come on, talk to these ladies. They're really nice and they're pro-choice."

Then Gloria showed that she really knew how to make someone feel special. "Hey, I've got a great radio talk show for you to do, and you're going to be the only one they have on. None of these other people—" she pointed to the stage "—will be on it. Just you."

Gloria and I are now on opposite sides of the abortion issue, but I found her to be a woman with a sweet and gracious heart. She's the type of woman I admire. I could tell she was hard-core, that she had overcome some rough spots in her lifetime, but that she had used these to create a career of looking out for the underdog, from the time she convinced Patty Hearst to leave the terrorists to the time she stood up for the victims during the O. J. Simpson trial.

"You've got to come to California," she told me as we parted for the day.

"Sure," I said. "Why not?"

CHAPTER 4
California Scheming

Nine days later, I was in Santa Monica. Gloria had paid my way, telling me, "You need to come to California for some rest, some sun, and some R & R."

We went to fancy restaurants and saw the sights. It was a great time, but I almost blew it right from the start. After I had been there for just a few days, I asked Gloria what she really thought about abortion, and Gloria told me that she had gotten an illegal one.

"You know, I think abortion's wrong," I said.

Gloria was silent, then excused herself. The next thing I knew, her secretary came out and said, "Get your coat."

"Where are we going?" I asked.

"I'm taking you back to your hotel. Gloria thinks she's been pushing you too hard. You can relax for the rest of the day."

It was only 10 A.M.

Jane Roe Comes Out

Gloria must have decided to overlook my bizarre statement, because the next day I got a call from her. "We're going to have a little news conference at our office," she said. "Would you like to join us?"

How could I refuse a woman who was giving me a paid vacation? "Sure," I said.

The "little news conference" turned out to be a media extravaganza. As I walked up to Gloria's office building, I was shocked by the camera trucks parked outside. Cameramen and crews blocked the hallways and were so busy, they looked like they were interviewing each other. It was the weirdest thing I've ever seen.

I thought, *There must be some really big celebrity in town to cause all this commotion. But who?*

Once I finally got to her office, Gloria asked me if I had any comments ready.

"Should I?" I asked, petrified.

"Oh, yes, you should always have some press comments ready. Tell you what. You just write something down, and I'll have my secretary type it up and make copies so the press can read it. Okay?"

And that was my preparation for my first big press conference. In the hour before we went on the air, I scribbled a few lines and handed them to Gloria. Gloria walked to the back and returned about twenty minutes later with a typed version. I noticed that when the secretary had finished typing my words, they extended to several paragraphs, even though I had written only a few sentences.

"What do I do with this?" I asked Gloria, seeing how my comments had grown.

"We'll hand out copies to the press, and then you can read it on the air."

"Why do I have to say my comments if the press is gonna read it?" I asked. That's how naive I was.

"Well, they just like to hear you say it in your own words."

"But these aren't my words—you changed everything!"

I was a handful for Gloria, but she was extremely patient and understanding. Even so, I'm sure I pushed her patience to the limit. I just didn't have a clue about how things were done, and up till now, that was always held against me. Gloria was the first person willing to invest the time to teach me.

"Did I really say this?" I asked Gloria, pointing to the sheet.

"Absolutely. I heard you say every word of it."

"I don't remember writing it."

"Well, I heard you say some of that back in Washington."

I had been drunk enough between then and the time I was in Washington that I was willing to believe her. Even if it wasn't true, I was willing to trust her.

I decided to slip out to have a cigarette and to collect my thoughts. After climbing over kneeling cameramen and walking around reporters and sound crews, I finally made it outside. There were news trucks everywhere with satellite dishes and booms sticking high into the air. I leaned over to talk to a man who was taping down some wires and asked him, "What is everybody here for?"

The man laughed. "Gloria has put together the biggest news conference of the year."

I felt my face redden. "Really? How'd she do that?"

"She brought Jane Roe to Los Angeles. Aren't you here for that?"

I didn't know what to say! "Kinda," I said.

"What paper are you with?" he asked skeptically.

"I'm . . . from Dallas."

I dropped my cigarette and got out of there!

The entire experience was surreal. A little over a week before, I was completely ignored. Now the national and international press were jammed into Gloria's offices just to meet me! I was terrified.

I fought my way back into Gloria's offices, stepping over camera bags and thankful that, for the next five minutes at least, I could remain anonymous. Now that I knew I was the focus of this mess, I was even more nervous about my comments, so I read them over again and again, amazed at how my few sentences had stretched so far.

The press conference finally started. Gloria called the media together, then built me up like a bona fide celebrity. *Where'd she get all this?* I thought when she began describing me to the press.

I read my comments—poorly, and without much energy—but I got through them. The press was very gentle and gracious with follow-up questions; not a single reporter threw a hardball my way. And Gloria was there to steer me around any tricky comments that might slip out unintentionally.

Twenty minutes later, several members of the press asked us to lunch.

Jane Roe was "out."

"I'm Gonna Make You Shine"

I went to sleep that night feeling warm, as if I had walked out of a cold fog and into the sunlight. I had found a woman who was willing to spend her hard-earned money to help me out. I was touched that Gloria thought enough of me to organize this hoopla, even though it caught me by surprise.

Though I felt increasingly alienated from the proabortion movement, I was willing to hang on because of Gloria. Besides, where else could I go? Gloria tried to help me through this, telling me that the proabortion leaders weren't going to be friendly—at least not to me.

The hostility of the proabortion crowd was hard to get used to! Several weeks before the march, I had spoken with an abortion clinic director. She looked at my feet and said, "Are you going to march with your black suede pumps, Norma?"

"I don't know, can I? You know I've never been to a march. I don't know what to wear."

"Well, I recommend that you wear your black suede pumps."

Until somebody else set me straight, I didn't realize she was making fun of me. There was no way I could walk across Washington in pumps!

That's the way I was treated—occasionally held up as a useful figurehead when the camera lights were on, but made fun of as soon as the crowds went away. Though the pro-lifers saw me as their nemesis, the one responsible for killing all the babies, those on "my side" looked at me as nothing but an inconvenient nuisance, a woman who had to be tolerated.

I had run away from home when I was just ten years old, I had worked as a bartender for most of my life, and at one point I even made a living as a carnival barker (not exactly the type of person you'd want to showcase a movement). But Gloria was willing to look past all that and teach me how to behave in the strange world of press releases, news conferences, and interviews. Because of her acceptance and patience, I still love her to this day.

"Norma," Gloria would say, "you're a diamond in the rough, but I'm gonna make you shine."

CHAPTER 5

The Shadow Plaintiff

People are usually surprised to learn that the *Roe v. Wade* decision was many hours old before I even heard about it. I came home from work—the first day I had been able to work in years, due to depression—and picked up the evening paper. Connie was taking a shower while I read the newspaper. Some newsbreak in the Watergate scandal had captured most of the ink, but in the lower right-hand corner of the *Dallas Times Herald* I noticed a news item announcing a Supreme Court decision about abortion.

Could this be me? I thought. The words announcing the Court's decision gripped me. It *was* me! I had won!

And yet it seemed so strange. I had already delivered my baby and placed her for adoption, so it really wasn't relevant to me—I couldn't abort a child who had already been born. In the article, I was referred to only through my pseudonym, Jane Roe, so even though they were talking about me, it felt like they were talking about someone else.

But I had won. There was some satisfaction in that, anyway.

Of course, you might well be wondering how I could have been so far removed. Why wasn't I at the Supreme Court when the case was argued on my behalf, for instance?

As soon as Sarah Weddington had my name on the affidavit, I had served my purpose. She called me back, all right—four months after my child was born.

"Sarah," I said. "I had a baby *four months ago.* Where were you then?" I didn't hear from Sarah again. She had said everything was going to be okay and that she would be there, but she wasn't.

This lack of relationship was not exactly a disappointment to me. Though Sarah had passed herself off as my friend, in reality she used me. When I sat down with her and discussed the possibility of getting an abortion, Sarah knew where I could get one, because she had gotten one herself three years before. When I asked her if the court's decision would come in time for me to get an abortion, she gave an evasive answer. And she did so with the full understanding that it would come way too late to help me.

If Sarah Weddington was so interested in abortion, why didn't she tell me where she got hers? Because I was of no use to her unless I was pregnant. She needed a pregnant woman who would sign the affidavit. If she told me how and where to get an abortion (or introduced me to people who knew, since, as a lawyer, she might have to cover herself), she wouldn't have a plaintiff. And without a plaintiff, somebody else might get their case before the Supreme Court first. That's why Sarah actually tried to talk me out of getting an illegal abortion in Mexico, as she had done.

Debbie Nathan, a proabortion writer, wrote in *the Texas Observer* (September 25, 1995): "By not effectively informing [Norma] of [where she could get an abortion], the feminists who put together *Roe v. Wade* turned McCorvey into Choice's sacrificial lamb—a necessary one, perhaps, but a sacrifice even so."

I never signed up to become a sacrificial lamb for anyone; I was just a young woman who needed help and who turned to the wrong people. After I gave up my child for adoption, I spent years searching the faces of children I passed on the streets and in supermarkets.

Is that her? I'd ask myself. *Could that be my child?*

"I'm Jane Roe"

"What's so interesting in the paper?" Connie asked as she walked around the corner, combing her hair. She had caught me staring and knew that a newspaper was not something I usually meditated over.

"They've legalized abortion."

I knew Connie was Roman Catholic, and I knew how the Church felt about abortion, so I was hesitant to tell Connie the whole truth. I wanted to feel her out first before I let her know the case had any personal significance.

"What do you think about that?" I asked her.

Connie shrugged. "I think that's great."

I downed a couple of beers to work up my nerve, then finally said, "You know, I'm the woman they call Jane Roe. That was my case that went to the Supreme Court."

Connie scoffed. "Yeah, and I'm the queen of England."

"Well, Queenie, shake my hand."

Connie looked at me skeptically, then held my eyes. She knew me well enough to know I wasn't lying. When I saw Connie's look of disbelief melt into the expression of a trusting and caring friend, I felt like a huge weight had fallen off my shoulders. Besides Sarah Weddington and my father, Connie was the first person to know about my role as Jane Roe.

It would remain a carefully guarded secret for almost a decade.

"They Say Abortion Is Killing Babies!"

A number of years later, I read in the newspaper about an abortion clinic being bombed. *Why would anyone want to do that?* I thought.

I read the entire article and was surprised when one of the bombers referred to "baby killing" going on inside the clinic. I had never been inside a clinic and could not imagine what the man was talking about, but that night, I had a dream in which I saw little babies lying around with daggers in their hearts. It was a horrific vision and I kept Connie up for hours, trying to figure out what it meant.

The next morning, I realized I needed to make some sort of sense out of this abortion business. I was Jane Roe, after all. What, really, had I done?

"You know, Connie," I said, fishing for her input, "here in the paper this person says that abortion is just killing little babies. What do you think?"

"Well, it's not a baby. It's just a piece of tissue that they remove, that's all."

"Do you think it's human?"

"Oh, no."

Connie's words didn't convince me. The dreams of babies being slaughtered kept up for some time.

Well, how do they kill a baby inside a mother's stomach, anyway? I couldn't get the thought out of my mind. I realize it sounds very naive, especially for a woman who had already conceived and delivered three children. Though I had seen and experienced more than my share of the world, there were some things about which I still didn't have a clue—and this was one of them. Ironically enough, Jane Roe may have known less about abortion than almost anyone else.

Eventually, I realized I needed to go to an abortion clinic and see an abortion actually performed. If my case had made abortion legal, I figured I should know what was going on.

During the late seventies, when I was working to pass the Equal Rights Amendment, I finally visited an abortion clinic for the first time, the Routh Street Women's Clinic. Abortion clinics often serve as centers for various (mostly liberal) political causes, and the ERA was certainly one cause that found vast support within the abortion community.

It was a bit scary for me even to go through the front door. I was invited in and I obliged, but when the director asked me, "Would you like a tour?" I answered, "I don't think so" a little too quickly, surprising her. The thought scared me. Because of what I had read in the paper, I envisioned seeing dead babies lying all over the place, so I did my best to stay in the front offices. I just didn't have the nerve to go in any farther.

Not until my two-year stay in California did I eventually get up the nerve to see an actual suction machine. I don't know what I expected, but since I had "come out," I knew I needed to show some interest, so when a clinic director told me she wanted me to see her new machine, I agreed to the full clinic tour.

It was almost as funny as it was sad. The clinic director acted like she was showing me a new sofa. "Look," she said, "this is our new suction machine!"

What was I supposed to say? "Looks like it'll really pull those babies out of there"? "Nice, stainless steel. Matches the table very well"? Call me cynical, but her excitement, even then, struck me as bizarre. I didn't feel excited looking at that machine. I just felt nauseous.

I still had not seen an abortion, and now, looking at that machine, I realized I did not really want to.

The clinic director was less than pleased by my lack of enthusiasm. Word would soon spread around the abortion world that Norma McCorvey was nothing but trouble.

CHAPTER 6

Leaning

"*Lean on me* instead of leaning on the drugs and booze," Gloria said to me on many occasions. I still don't know why she would spend all this effort on an addict, but she did.

She had been warned otherwise. Plenty of leaders had gone up to her and said, "Don't have anything to do with that McCorvey woman. She's bad news. You'll regret it." But Gloria didn't listen.

One time Gloria called me on the phone and admitted, "There are so many people against you, it's no wonder you are what you are (a sassy, outspoken, take-no-guff type of woman), but I don't care what they say. I'm your Yiddish mama and I'll take care of you. You're going to shine like you should have shined a long time ago."

Having this as her goal, Gloria was clearly swimming upstream. Sarah Weddington and company didn't want me to shine. I was chosen because they needed someone who would sign the paper and fade into the background, never coming out and always keeping silent.

Ideally, in their minds, I would have just stayed quiet, got on with my life, and quietly suffered, perhaps eventually committing suicide. I would have been much more useful to them (not to mention famous) if I had died young. As long as I was alive, I was a danger. I might speak out. I could be unpredictable.

And I was.

A Tap on the Shoulder

Gloria and I went to an L.A. fund-raiser in the summer of 1989. Sarah Weddington was speaking on behalf of an abortion advocacy group, and we wanted to hear what she had to say. I had never heard Sarah give a formal speech, and I was looking forward to her talk.

We almost didn't get in—Sarah and Gloria don't get along too well. I never found out why, as Gloria isn't the type to trash people behind their backs, but it was obvious to me that no love was lost between the two.

I ended up getting a second-row seat, right in front of the stage. Shortly after I sat down, I caught Sarah's eyes. She smiled, then recognized who I was. The smile quickly faded into an icy glare.

Gloria and I waited patiently as Sarah finished her talk, then we stood up and got in line to greet her. Sarah saw me coming and turned her back, pretending she didn't see me, but it was obvious that she had. Gloria looked at me and then dropped her eyes—it was her way of telling me she was sorry. We both knew what was going on.

I didn't want to see Sarah that badly, but nobody is going to slight me like that! I walked up to her and tapped her on the shoulder.

"Excuse me, Sarah," I said. "It's Norma. I'm your former client."

I'll admit my greeting was more of an accusation than a hello. Sarah had told me she would be there for me after my baby was born, but she never was—at least not after she got my signature. Yet for all those years, I had loved Sarah. I was proud of her. She was professional, educated, accomplished—everything I wasn't. But, somehow, our lives had connected for something that ended up making history.

But we could never get over the gulf that lay between us. We had a big disagreement back in the mid-to late eighties as NBC worked to put together the movie on my life. Sarah thought I should give all the money away, and I thought she was crazy. "You get five thousand dollars for one lecture," I protested. "I could use half of that just to pay some overdue bills."

Sarah charged NBC $120 an hour to serve as a consultant, but said I should be paid less, because if I got paid more, I'd be considered a woman of "ill repute." This got me so angry I had Connie call her office to make sure I had heard her correctly. I've worked every petty job to make a living—from cleaning out apartments (on one occasion, finding a dead body!) to construction work. And now that I was finally being offered some money for something that didn't have me breaking my back, Sarah seemed to resent it.

Not that Sarah had a problem chasing money when the opportunity presented itself. In 1995 she ran into some controversy of her own when she was chastised for lobbying on behalf of a New England power plant seeking to dump radioactive waste near a largely Hispanic, poor community in West Texas. A number of people in the feminist community have sought to link environmental contamination with breast cancer, and Sarah's willingness to throw her principles to the wind for a big payoff made me wonder whether her insistence that I give up all my money for the movie didn't come from Sarah's own guilty conscience.

Even Sarah couldn't wreck the experience, however, as the movie was a dream come true for me. I always wanted to be a Hollywood actress, another Rita Hayworth, Mitzi Gaynor, or Lauren Bacall. (What young girl hasn't had such a dream at one time or another?) They chose Holly Hunter to play me, so I never really got my chance.

Being Used

Gloria's unconditional acceptance helped me weather slights like Sarah's. Apart from the fact that Gloria knew how to do seventy-two hours worth of media in a twenty-four-hour day, we had a lot of fun. We'd get in her Mercedes, put Bob Marley in her tape deck, then I'd hold on for dear life as Gloria drove while speaking on her car phone. She never traded paint with another car (at least not while I was with her), but we came close enough on several occasions to exchange greetings.

We traveled all over the country—Chicago, New Orleans, Los Angeles, Washington, D.C., you name it. It was an entirely new world for me. We came back to the nation's capital during the oral arguments for *Webster v. Reproductive Health Services* in 1989 (in which the Court allowed certain minor restrictions on abortion).

A reporter walked toward us inside the Supreme Court building and stopped when he saw us. "I know who you are!" he exclaimed.

I turned around.

"No, the other woman. You're Gloria Allred, media junkie."

"Let me tell you something, sugar," I said. "How old are you?"

"Twenty-eight."

"Well, do you want to die right here, or would you like to live to twenty-nine?" I was ready to tackle this guy on the spot. Gloria had taken care of me, and now I was going to get a chance to take care of her. Unfortunately, I never got my chance. That young stud saw I meant business and got himself out of there!

That evening, I looked around me and couldn't believe where I was. From cleaning out low-rent apartments, I was now staying at the Washington Hilton—courtesy of this alleged media junkie—and I had never seen anything like it. I had a television and phone in my bathroom, more freshly laundered towels than I could possibly use in a day, and somebody who even made my bed.

Sometimes a staff member would knock on my door for no reason except to ask me if I needed anything. I had never received such royal treatment in all my life. I didn't even know such luxury existed.

Gloria never quit looking out for me. I'd get a phone call from her room at odd hours. "Just calling to see how you're doing," she'd say.

"Don't worry, Gloria," I'd reassure her. "I'm not at the bar, okay?"

In front of the media, Gloria has a tremendously tough exterior—she has to. But inside, she's like a little kitten, and we had tremendous fun together. Plenty of people came up to me and warned me, "You know, Gloria's just using you."

"Well, she's not using me any worse than Sarah Weddington used me," I replied. As long as her "using" me involved taking me to places like the Washington Hilton, I was ready to be used! These people should have been there when I was growing up and met some of the characters who had *really* used me. It was no accident that when I was a girl in reform school I had organized an "I hate all adults" club! If they had met the man who broke into my childhood innocence with his lustful attacks, if they had known the man who got me pregnant and then beat me up for it—then they would know what it was like to be used. Then they would understand that Gloria would never fit in that camp. She fed me, she arranged for us to stay in nice places, and she always had a smile on her face. That was a whole lot more than I could say about most people in my life at the time.

Rescue

I remember when I saw a rescue with Gloria while I was in L.A. News of Randall Terry's new organization, Operation Rescue, had become an obsession with the proabortion movement, as we could sense the momentum slipping out of our hands. We liked to say on camera that Rescue did the pro-life movement more harm than good, but thoughtful people were moved by the profiles in courage that took place in front of abortion clinics all across the country. People of all ages sat peacefully in front of clinic doors as counselors on the sidewalk asked clients not to go in. Dr. Bernard Nathanson, a former atheist and abortion doctor turned pro-life advocate, cites his experience watching a rescue as the impetus for him to reconsider the Christian faith.

As Gloria and I walked the streets of L.A., I was surprised that we didn't see more people. When we turned a corner and reached the rescue, however, there were *tons* of people. It was like a street fair, shoulder to shoulder, with people bumping into one another, squeezed between the surrounding buildings. I thought the whole city must have shifted to this one street.

There were policemen everywhere—on horses, backing up buses, on foot, you name it.

"Oi vey," Gloria said—Yiddish for "my goodness."

The press recognized us and started running up to us. "Don't say anything until we start the press conference," Gloria warned.

"Got it," I said.

The police managed to keep the antichoicers on one side of the street and the pro-choicers on the other. Screaming was coming from both sides.

Finally, the rescuers started approaching the abortion clinic, crawling slowly on their hands and knees. On cue, the police began closing in from both sides.

"We can't see anything from here," Gloria said. "Let's get a better view."

We ended up going through a building and getting onto the roof, only to find that our view was obstructed.

"Come on, let's go over there." Gloria pointed.

I couldn't figure out how she intended for us to get onto that other building. I certainly didn't want to go back down and then up another building, so we decided on a shortcut—we would jump from one roof to the next!

"I don't know if I can make it," Gloria said. The jump wasn't that far, but at three stories high, the building was tall enough to be intimidating.

"Let me go first," I offered.

I reached over the side of the building and grabbed a drainpipe, which I used to steady myself as I stepped two feet up onto the next wall.

I made it safely.

"Here's my hand," I told Gloria. "Take it and don't look down."

"I've got to look down," Gloria insisted.

"No, don't, you'll get scared."

"I have to."

She looked down.

I reached out my hand and managed to grasp her, thankful she was light and thin. We got up on top of that building and settled in for the view.

It was crazy. Some people were lying down in front of the abortion clinic doors, cops closing in with riot gear. Not a single rescuer resisted. None of them helped the cops, mind you—each rescuer made the police officer drag him or her away—but there was no need for the riot gear.

I don't know if the cops were upset because they had to drag these people or what, but it became clear that with each passing rescuer, the protesters were being treated worse and worse, like sacks of dirt. If a pile of horse manure stood in the path of a rescuer being dragged away, the police never bothered to divert their angle—the protester was pulled right through it. With the yanking, shoving, and dropping going on as the police threw rescuers into the buses, I was certain that many of them were suffering pulled muscles, or worse.

"How do you like that," I told Gloria, laughing. "Going through horse manure and having to take a bath before you get thrown in jail!"

"Norma," Gloria said, "they don't get a bath. They go in there smelling like that for a long time."

I got sick to my stomach. All of a sudden, this wasn't so funny.

"I want to go down," I said. "I don't want to be here no more. Let's just leave."

I never actually talked to a rescuer. Gloria warned me, "We have to be very careful when we go around them." She was afraid for my safety, so we kept our distance, despising and ridiculing them from afar.

Never would I have dreamed that I could even consider joining them.

CHAPTER 7

Working the Business

I ended up spending almost two years in California, but eventually I came back to live in the Dallas area.

Life had changed. People knew I was Jane Roe. I had done the interviews, I had had my picture taken, I had given speeches, attended marches, you name it.

But I never did fit in. I spoke too bluntly. I didn't try to act like a lady. I was honest when something bothered me. That got some people upset, so I returned to Texas.

Back in Dallas, I knew I could not return to construction work, which I had been doing before I left for L.A. When you leave a job like that for a couple of years, it's doubly hard to go back. And I didn't relish the thought of returning to cleaning, either. Now in my forties, I was not looking forward to being twenty floors off the ground, cleaning windows.

Shortly after I got back from California, a doctor approached me about opening up the "Jane Roe Women's Center." He said he would bankroll the entire operation, hoping to make the

JRWC the political arm of the abortion movement—sort of "finishing what I started," as he put it. We planned to gather information and put out a newsletter to let people in all fifty states know about pending legislation and elected officials' voting records.

It all sounded good to me. I figured I could push paper with the best of them, and at the same time, I could do something for the movement, so I accepted his offer and took an apartment in north Dallas, working to establish this political organization.

The JRWC never accomplished all that much, but it did usher me into another world. The doctor suggested that "while we work to get the center going," perhaps I would spend some time working at his abortion clinic. Nothing medical, mind you, but I could help out with marketing and making appointments.

"Sure!" I said, and that's how I ended up working for my first abortion clinic. For the next several years, abortion would be my life.

"Do You Realize Where You're At?"

Within weeks, I started drinking again. The day-to-day stress inside an abortion clinic is unbelievable. Women seeking an abortion can be incredibly demanding. One woman in particular was irate. She had just found out she was pregnant, her husband was in prison so he would know it couldn't be his, and she wanted an abortion *now*.

I was startled that many of these women never even struggled with the implications of what they were doing. They were very often panicked and in a hurry—not thinking, just acting. Abortion looked like the easiest way to undo everything. Most of the women I saw did not arrive at their "decision" after "careful consultation" with a doctor. Many of them could not remember whom they had slept with, or when; they just knew they were pregnant and they wanted the doctor to get rid of it.

Time after time, I sensed women were jumping the gun by immediately coming in for an abortion. I think that's why the twenty-four-hour waiting period proposed by pro-lifers became so controversial. *What's the big deal about waiting twenty-four hours?* most people would think. But when you want an abortion, you want it now. Twenty-four hours seems like forever.

I began to make enemies right away, thinking that women should at least get a fighting chance to understand what they were doing. I remember one afternoon in particular. A woman came up to the desk and said, "I am so terribly nervous, I can't fill out this form."

A patient behind her clicked her gum and said, "Don't worry about it. It's just like getting a tooth pulled."

"Excuse me?" I cut in. Then, to the woman who spoke first, I said, "Sugar, are you sure this is what you want to do? Do you realize where you're at? This isn't like visiting the dentist. This is an abortion clinic. If you go back there, they're going to take your baby away."

One of the clinic workers sitting behind me began loudly clearing her throat, then said, "Norma. Norma." I kept talking.

"Norma!"

I wasn't about to be stopped. I was just getting started. "Hasn't anyone explained to you what's going to happen?" I asked the client.

"Not really."

I wasn't surprised. "Let me explain something to you, girlfriend." I took her outside, ignoring the exclamations of disgust behind me, and explained the procedure, step-by-step.

The girl's face became so white I thought she was going to faint. She was horrified.

"Are you sure you know what you're doing?" I asked. "You're so young and cute. I don't want to see you get hurt."

The girl shook her head. She never responded to my question. She just turned away from the clinic and never came back.

Michel-man and Company

Just because I was working at the abortion clinic did not mean that my political activities died, however. I don't know why, but Gloria kept me active on the national scene. When David Souter was nominated for the Supreme Court, Gloria and I went to Washington, D.C., to sit on a panel with other proabortion leaders: Eleanor Smeal, Kate Michelman, Molly Yard, Faye Wattleton, the usual crowd.

I was a bit awed to be in the presence of these famous professional women and wanted to make a good impression. I saw a pin in Kate Michelman's lapel and complimented her on it. "What a great-looking pin, Kate," I said. "I have to get one of those."

Kate stared at me haughtily. "In case you don't know what this represents, Norma, it's the pin for the National Abortion Rights Action League."

Her tone set me off. "Well, whoop whoop tee do," I said. "Aren't you the articulate one?"

Gloria saw what was going on and quickly pulled me away. "Norma! Norma! I really *must* speak with you."

I told Gloria what I thought I ought to do to put Kate in her place, but Gloria convinced me that ignoring her would be better.

I'm glad she did.

Later, I was surprised at the animosity among all the leaders. As we sat at a table preparing to speak before the Senate panel, these women were throwing daggers at one another every chance they got. I had never seen such cold, hard stares in all my life.

Gloria had warned me about this, but I still could not get used to it. I have a quick temper and I take offense rather easily. Their attitude, I'm sorry to say, brought out the worst in me.

"Norma, don't put your elbows on the table," Eleanor Smeal corrected me. "It's not ladylike."

Clearly, I was an embarrassment to them.

"I thought you were a hard-core feminist," I countered. "Why should I try to be ladylike?"

Eleanor shot me a cold look.

The senators asked us to introduce ourselves and to state what we wanted placed in the public record. My temper had already been ignited by Kate's and Eleanor's condescension, so I started things off badly. "My name is Norma McCorvey, a.k.a. Jane Roe of *Roe v. Wade*. I am *the* Jane Roe. These other ladies think they should be, but they're not."

Sen. Joseph Biden was so shocked, he just about swallowed his tongue. He did not understand that my comments did not come in a vacuum. Allow me to explain.

After I had come out as Jane Roe, feminists regularly came up to me and said, "I don't know why they chose you. They could have chosen me." One woman approached me at a California rally, lifted her nose, and said, "They should have picked me. I'm much more familiar with the issues."

My lack of an Ivy League education bothered many of these professional women. One time, at a Dallas abortion clinic, I was painting a sign for an upcoming rally when a national leader from NOW came in and scolded me in front of everyone for doing "crappy" work. My crime? I had misspelled a word.

All right, so I don't have a Ph.D.! Does that mean people can treat me like dirt?

In general, the proabortion crowd resented the fact that Norma McCorvey was historically tied to legalized abortion. This growing resentment just sat inside my gut and made me bitter. I drank. I smoked. I cussed people out. But that never beat the bitterness, it just fed it. When Eleanor and Kate slighted me that day, years of frustration came out.

It wasn't pretty.

Sen. Strom Thurmond introduced himself and said, "I'd like to tell each one of you how lovely you all look today." You don't tell seven hard-core feminists how lovely they look when they have come to testify before a Senate panel! The women seated next to me wore strained smiles, but I cut in with, "Well, Senator, I like that tie you got on there, guy. Where'd you get that? You look right pretty yourself today."

The other senators laughed and laughed. They didn't know what to expect, but they sure didn't expect this.

Kate leaned forward to stare at me with disapproval, but I wasn't about to take anything more from her. "Save it, Michel-

man," I told her. "You all just think you're guys anyway. You said you had an abortion because your husband left you. Wasn't that a good reason to kill your baby?"

I'm sure Gloria wanted to slide underneath the table. "Norma," she said, "you're making this very difficult."

A World of Hurt

Of course, none of this was reported in the press. The media never wants to show the dark side or divisions in the abortion movement.

Afterward, I went back to my hotel room at the Washington Hilton, and I started laughing. In between sips of brandy alexanders, I kept saying to myself, *I might have looked like a hick, but I got that woman. I put her in her place.*

I wasn't surprised when the phone rang and I found Gloria on the other line. "Norma," she asked, "why did you say those things?"

The brandy alexanders had relaxed me. I wasn't about to apologize. "Gloria, I said those things because I felt like it."

This makes me sound like a hard, bitter lady, but let me open the window to my soul just a little bit. The truth is, I was hurting desperately. I had never come to grips with my three adoptions. What I wanted to say to Gloria was, "I already gave my babies away. Without anyone to be responsible for, I don't have anything to lose. What do I care what people think of me?"

When I looked at the leaders of the abortion movement, ostensibly working for women's rights while making women like me feel like dirt, I just couldn't take it. I'm not proud of my actions, but putting me with those leaders was like hitting two flints together—sparks were inevitable.

I was emotionally bleeding in front of everyone, but nobody knew how to stop it. In light of this, I guess it's not so surprising that I was not invited to the White House for the Twentieth Anniversary Celebration of *Roe v. Wade* in 1993. If you burn your bridges, you can't expect to walk over them again. But it is ironic that Jane Roe was not there to celebrate the case that bore her name.

Perhaps it was for the best. The year 1993 was during what I call my "shame period." My religious upbringing was wearing on me, so though I spouted the proper pro-choice rhetoric, deep in my gut I knew my identity as Jane Roe was nothing to be proud of. Women's rights were one thing; abortion, well, that was something else altogether.

Not surprisingly, the pro-lifers did their best not to let me forget what I had done, and this had something to do with the shame I felt. Once it became known that I was Jane Roe, Connie and I opened up the curtains one morning to find baby clothes scattered across our front yard. Those tiny dresses and baby socks just about ripped my heart out.

I would go to the mailbox and find photographs of cut-up fetuses that turned my stomach. Dolls with their arms or heads pulled off were routinely thrown into our yard or on the front porch.

We tried to pretend that this didn't bother us. We'd laugh it off: "Oh, what will they think of next?" But after a while, it gets to you. It really does.

Sometimes, though, I wondered if the pro-choice group wasn't doing some of this "decorating." They did not exactly relish the thought that I was Jane Roe, and they knew how weak I was. It didn't take a surgeon to recognize the suicide scars on my arms. They knew I was a drunk, a pill taker, a drug abuser, and that one small push might be enough on any given day or in any given hour to encourage me to take my own life.

When you live with a deep shame and that shame is compounded with vivid images such as children's clothing and desecrated dolls, and your psyche is already rendered weak by drug abuse, you're a tragedy waiting to happen. There are people who delight in preying on the weak. I was clearly weak. I needed help.

If you think I had problems getting along with the feminists, however, that was nothing compared to my interactions with the Rescuers—and with Flip Benham in particular.

CHAPTER 8

"Miss McCorvey, You're Responsible for the Deaths of Thirty-five Million Children!"

The first time I met Flip face-to-face was during a book signing for my book *I Am Roe*. It was a hot June night in Dallas, and my appearance had been announced via flyers, posters, newspaper notices, and the radio, so it was not hard for the antis to be informed and prepared.

Rescue was out in full force. Ironically, it was Ronda Mackey—the woman whose daughter eventually got me to church—who distributed a list of tough questions that people could ask me during the open question-and-answer time. After I became a Christian, I finally saw a copy of one of these sheets:

Questions to Ask Norma McCorvey

(Don't let people see you looking at this paper)

1. What happened to the baby that you were trying to abort?

2. Have you had an abortion since *Roe v. Wade*? Have you used your "right to choose"? Why or why not?

3. Ninety-five percent of women who had an abortion said if they had any other choice, they would have taken it (survey done by Nurturing Network). You were in a difficult situation when you were pregnant during *Roe*. What would you have needed in order to give life to your child, or to not want an abortion?

4. The Alan Guttmacher Institute determined that over 90 percent of the women who had an abortion suffered complications (physical and/or emotional). What are you doing to help or counsel women after the abortion—especially those who are hurt from it?

There were many questions like this, but the last one may have been the most intriguing:

9. It seems the abortion industry has just been using you from the beginning. They used your sad situation to get abortion legalized, then they didn't even call you when the case was won in the Supreme Court. They didn't have anything to do with you until the *Webster* decision, when it seemed like *Roe* would be overturned. Have you ever intellectually questioned how the abortion industry operates, or the arguments they use? Have they—the feminists and abortion providers—listened to you and changed anything?

I think you can see why Ronda eventually ended up being so successful in reaching out to me!

The book signing was held at the Cafe Society, a small but charming restaurant that serves overpriced (but delicious) chicken dishes in a valiant attempt to bring France to the Dallas area. The restaurant owners are outspokenly liberal in their efforts, and accepted donations to the CHOICE foundation during my signing. Their newsletter states that the Cafe is "about breaking down false barriers that separate humanity. Cafe Society is where people recognize and respect one another as individuals."

This respect did not necessarily extend to pro-lifers, apparently. Unknown to me, Ronda Mackey and Wendy Wright were outside the cafe, picketing my appearance. One of the cafe's security guards walked up to Ronda and Wendy and told them to leave.

"This is a public sidewalk," Ronda protested. "I don't have to leave."

"It's private property," the guard countered, shoving Ronda into the street. A sidewalk is not private property, of course, but the guard was determined to get these women out of there. He walked over and shoved Wendy into the street as well.

"You're assaulting me!" Wendy protested. "Are you assaulting me?"

"Yes," he said.

"You would use violence against a woman?"

"Yes."

"You're not a man or you wouldn't be pushing a woman around," Ronda countered.

"Would you like me to show you how much of a man I am?"

"NO!"

The guard would not stop shoving, so eventually the police were called, and an officer informed the guard that he could not prevent Wendy and Ronda from picketing on the sidewalk. He also issued a citation to the guard for shoving the women after both said they would like to press charges.

The women had stayed outside for some time, when the guard asked Wendy, "Do you have any kids?"

"No."

He turned to Ronda. "Do you have any kids?"

"Yes."

"You'd better think twice about going through with the charges."

"Excuse me?"

"If you have kids, you'd better think twice about going through with the charges."

"Is that a threat?" Ronda took an involuntary step backward. She was shocked.

"You'd better watch out for them," the guard repeated.

"The Antis Are Here!"

Inside, the cafe was pretty full and people were still trying to crowd in when one of the local abortion workers warned me, "Norma, don't be frightened, but it looks like some antichoicers have shown up. They're causing some kind of confrontation outside."

"I'm not frightened," I said. "If they want to buy a book, let 'em!"

The woman laughed. "I doubt they'll come here to buy books."

"Whatever."

About five minutes later I heard her say, "Oh, my goddess. Oh, my goddess. There's Operation Rescue!" In a sarcastic tone she added, "I wonder where Flippie is?"

Though I had never met Flip in person, I had seen him on television. I decided to ignore Rescue's presence, gave my short presentation, and then opened the floor for questions.

Ronda's "tough questions" sheet immediately became obvious.

"Miss McCorvey, is it true that you sued Gloria Allred over a fund-raiser in Los Angeles, California?"

"No, ma'am, that's not true," I said, then thought to myself, *Where could she have come up with that?*

My anger started to rise. When my temper gets up, I become dangerous. But before I could really react, I heard a booming voice in the back of the cafe: "Norma McCorvey! You ought to be ashamed of yourself!"

I felt my knees grow weak. The voice was a deep, powerful one. I saw Flip, recognized him as the leader of Operation Rescue, and was startled that he looked so intimidating.

"You are responsible for the deaths of thirty-five million babies! How dare you desecrate their blood by selling a book?"

People started gathering around to protect me, but it had the opposite effect. I felt suffocated. I don't like crowds. At the time, I didn't even like people much, and here they were, all around me, with one of them booming out his judgment of me.

I looked back and saw Connie. "Are you okay?" I asked.

"I'm fine. How are you doing?"

"Okay."

"We're not having dinner here," Connie said.

"All right."

"As soon as you sign that book, we're gone."

There was some scrambling and jostling in the crowd outside the cafe, and Connie and I figured we'd better get moving right away. Remember, our house had been shot up just a few years before. An abortionist, David Gunn, had been shot and killed in Florida rather recently, and we were understandably gun-shy.

Connie shielded me with her body whenever I walked in front of exposed windows as we made our way toward the parking garage. I saw rescuers going around the building in front of us, but I told myself, *Surely, if they're going to shoot me, they're not going to do it in front of a crowd.*

There has never been a single instance of a member of Operation Rescue who used violence during a protest; but we spent so much time describing them as violent radicals, we had begun to convince ourselves that they really were dangerous fanatics.

Connie and I finally made it to our car and drove off. Ten minutes later, I was still shaking, hoping I'd never see that Flip Venom again.

A Shattered Psyche

To be fair to Flip, I had given him even more than he had dished out to me. Yes, he had been forceful, but I had been downright crude. When I worked at A to Z, I left some particularly heinous phone messages on his answering machine.

"Hey, Flip, we're through killing little baby boys and girls today. We're thinking of having a barbecue with them, but we need a recipe, so how about faxing one over?" We were stoned out of our minds, and, back then, we thought this was great fun. It never occurred to me that Ronda Mackey, the woman who would walk up the aisle with me on the day I was converted, was the one who had to listen to these messages.

"How could you do it, Norma?" people ask me now. "How could you possibly say something so cruel?"

The only answer I can give is that working in an abortion clinic, combined with drugs, had robbed me of my feelings. One particular abortion set it all off.

In 1991 I was working behind the desk at an abortion clinic when a woman who was about six months pregnant walked into our office.

"You're in the wrong place, honey," I said. "The OB-GYN clinic is down the hall. This is the place for abortions."

"Oh, no, I'm in the right place," she said. Her voice had a startling lack of emotion, considering what she was saying.

"But you're showing," I protested.

Her tone was insistent. "I know what I want, and what I want is an abortion."

I left her standing there and went to the back to get a cigarette. You have to understand, when situations like these arose, I felt responsible. My name was on that affidavit. It was my pseudonym, Jane Roe, that had been used to create the "right" to abortion out of legal thin air. But Sarah Weddington and Linda Coffee had never told me that what I was signing would allow women to use abortion as a form of birth control. We talked about truly desperate and needy women, not women already wearing maternity clothes.

The doctor at A to Z finally saw the woman who was six months pregnant and instructed the nurses to prepare her with laminaria.

"You've got to be kidding," I protested. "She's wearing maternity clothes! There's got to be movement. And you're going to do an abortion?"

They just looked at me with confused condescension. "What's your problem? This is an abortion clinic. Abortions are what we do."

"I can't handle this," I said. "I'm outta here."

"Fine, take the afternoon off."

But I couldn't get the woman out of my mind. I kept calling the clinic. "Is she still there?"

"Yes."

I just couldn't believe that a woman who was so far along that she had to wear maternity clothes would be coming in for an abortion. I started drinking and didn't stop for almost two weeks. Finally, I got up the nerve to go back to the clinic, reminding myself that she wasn't our normal client.

It never occurred to me that she would come back that day for her two-week follow-up.

She looked terrible. She was pale, unusually thin, weary, placid, and her eyes looked swollen. She looked like someone who should be checking into a hospital. After taking one look at me, she said, "I don't want no part of her."

"That goes double for me," I said. "How could you do that?"

"Mind your own (expletive) business," she said. "Besides, you've got a lot of room to talk. You're standing right here doing it."

"You got that right," I said. I couldn't deny that she was right, so I immediately left the office and stayed out for another week or so.

You see, abortions are an inherently dehumanizing business. You have to let a part of your soul die, or at least go numb, to stay in practice. In fact, I think it would be helpful if I take a chapter to tell you exactly what goes on behind the abortion clinic doors. Maybe then you will be able to understand what I was going through.

I'm not trying to make excuses; I just want to share the facts.

CHAPTER 9

A Day in the Life

To give you just some idea of what it's like to work in an abortion clinic, I'd like to walk you through a typical procedure. Of course, every procedure varies, depending on how long a woman has been pregnant; but let's say for the sake of argument that she's about ten weeks along.

In the last clinic I worked at, the doctor would offer the woman "counseling" that went something like this.

"You want abortion?"

"Yes."

"You sign here, I give abortion."

At first, Arnie never explained the mechanics of abortion, never went over the risks of abortion, and never discussed the woman's individual situation. Arnie insisted that women did not want counseling. "They not care," he said. "They want it over with. A problem with them, that is all."

"Don't you even tell them how it's done?" I asked.

"Oh no. She will figure it out when she is in there."

"But women in that room can get distraught!" I protested. I had worked at A to Z. I knew what could happen.

"If so, I will tell them how hard it was for me to go to medical school," Arnie answered.

"I'm sure they really want to hear that, Arnie."

This complete lack of counseling really bothered me. I remember seeing all these young women in the waiting room and thinking, *They have a right to know what's going to happen to their bodies. Abortion is a serious procedure. If the doctor goes within a quarter of an inch of the uterus, he could puncture it and a woman might bleed to death.*

But as long as she had the money, any woman could get an abortion at our clinic, provided she was willing to sign a waiver that said she was doing this of her own free will after "consultation with her physician."

What kind of woman would put up with this? you might ask. In all honesty, abortion has a way of reducing so-called women into girls. In all our proabortion rhetoric, we talked about "women's rights," but you've never seen as many teddy bears as you'll see in one week at an abortion clinic.

To be fair to Arnie, his counseling eventually improved. We insisted on it. But it was never even remotely what I would call sufficient.

Getting It Done

After "counseling," we would lead the patient into the back room, where she would typically wait for an hour or two, then we would take her to a dressing room, where she would put on a surgical gown, but leave her socks on. Then we'd help her up on the table, get her in position, and put her feet in the stirrups.

Once the patient was settled, we hit her with about 40 percent nitrous oxide. Though I have received no medical training, I routinely performed this function (as well as other medical acts, such as drawing blood). Most abortionists do not want to spend the money to pay a specialist.

It takes about ten minutes for the laughing gas to get into the bloodstream. After that, a nurse comes in and numbs the woman's cervix with a small needle. Then she would nod my way. My job was to talk to the women and get them to relax. I would usually resort to small talk.

"Do you ski?" I'd ask in winter.

"A little bit," a timid voice would reply.

"I hear that Angel Fire had so much snow dumped this morning that the skiing is just great. Won't it be fun to get out there and take a couple of runs real soon?"

"Yeah. Great."

I would do anything to get them to stay relaxed. When I saw them tense up, I'd say, "Think about the nicest thing you've ever seen. Got it? Good. Now tell me about it." Or: "Tell me about the prettiest dress you've ever owned."

During this time the doctor is dilating the patient's cervix with his instruments. He then begins scraping the uterus with an instrument that looks like a tongue depressor—those little wooden things doctors stick in your throat when they ask you to say "aaahhhh." Soon, a little bit of blood begins to trickle out of the woman's body, and the doctor inserts a cannula—a medical tube—into the vaginal canal.

Often this was the first time Arnie would address the patient directly. "Okay, machine may scare you. I have not talked to you because Norma is here to talk to you for me. She is my representative. If you have questions, talk to Norma."

Invariably, the woman would grab my hand—I learned to remove all my rings because many of those young women were very strong. I tried not to wince, even when their fingernails bit into my skin, drawing blood.

The doctor turned the machine on, the woman's body shook in rhythm with it, her legs began to quiver, and sometimes I had to hold her hips. If the woman was a squirmer, I would have to restrain her.

At least 80 percent of the women would try to look down at the end of the table, wondering if they could see anything, which is why our doctor always went in with the scalpel first. Once the baby was already cut up, there was nothing but blood and torn-up tissue for the woman to see.

When a later abortion was performed, workers had to piece the baby back together, and every major piece—head, torso, two legs, and two arms—had to be accounted for. One of our little jokes at the clinic was, "If you ever want to humble a doctor, hide a leg so he thinks he has to go back in."

Please understand, these were not abnormal, uncaring women working with me at the clinic. We were just involved in a bloody, dehumanizing business, all of us for our own reasons. Whether we were justifying our past advocacy (as I was), justifying a previous abortion (as many were), or whatever, we were just trying to cope—and if we couldn't laugh at what was going on, I think our minds would have snapped. It's not an easy thing trying to confuse a conscience that will not stay dead.

Women typically began crying as soon as the machine was shut off. Our standard line was, "Honey, you've just had fifteen milligrams of liquid Valium, and it's only natural that you should feel so emotional. Don't worry. It'll pass." We could *never* admit to the fact that she might be crying because she realized what she had just done to her baby.

We then wheeled the girl into recovery, put a pad on her, pulled the curtain to give her some privacy, then checked vital signs: blood pressure and pulse. Again, I was usually the one to do this.

I laugh about it now, but sometimes I would feel really ripped off by the doctor. Since I booked the abortions, I knew what he was getting paid for each one, but he bolstered his profits by hiring untrained help like me for six bucks an hour.

Then what kept me there? I got so attached to the women, I forgot all about the abortionist. In some ways, I felt I needed to be there to protect them and humanize the whole process. Your heart breaks for these young girls who come in hugging their teddy bears and other stuffed animals.

The other workers and I addressed these girls by their first names only, to help foster intimacy. We were their only solace during a very frightening three hours. Some of them held on to us for dear life. We would listen to them cry, listen to them pray, listen to them swear, listen to them beg their child for forgiveness.

After they had been in the recovery room for an hour or two, we would help the women clean up, get dressed, and try to get them to drink some juice and eat some crackers. I always stressed the importance of coming back for a two-week exam, in part because so many women skipped it. Many just couldn't bear to return to the scene.

We handed out their prescriptions, assured them that they had "done the right thing" and that "of course it wasn't really a baby; it was just a missed period," and sometimes dialed the phone for them if their hands were too shaky.

If the woman had a man who was waiting out front, she would usually try to clean up her face and put on a weak smile before she stepped outside. Women tended to be a little more honest with their mothers. I heard one young woman call her mom and say, "Mom, I just killed my baby. I'm so glad you never killed me!"

"You Know What I Saw"

I am not proud at all to admit that I also assisted in second-trimester abortions. These are much more difficult and harder on everyone—patient, doctor, and assistant. First, the woman has to go through the laminaria procedure. The laminaria is compressed seaweed, put together in the form of a stick (about the length of a toothpick) with a string on the end. The doctor places the laminaria inside the woman's body, and the laminaria begins to swell, opening her cervix and beginning to crush the child inside. Depending on how far along the mother is in her pregnancy, she may require several laminaria.

The late-term abortion proceeds similar to a first-trimester abortion. The doctor uses a scalpel to cut the baby up. Most women are sedated with general anesthesia, so the doctor can be as forceful as necessary without worrying about the patient's reaction.

I will always remember one second-trimester abortion. The young woman was very attractive, with fair skin, blue eyes, and slightly reddish hair; I'd guess she was around eighteen years old. She was so sweet and pleasant, not at all demanding, and a first-year student at a local college.

"I've heard I'll have to miss classes for two weeks," she told me. "I don't know how I'll ever make up the homework."

I laughed reassuringly. "Oh, no, honey; you can go back to school tomorrow. You just can't be sexually active for two weeks, and you'll need to take showers instead of baths during that time. Other than that, you'll be fine."

She smiled prettily and said, "Okay, how do we start?"

It was weird because she seemed so naive to be in this situation. When she first came in, she said she wasn't sure if she was pregnant, even though she had just entered her second trimester.

After we discussed prices, she decided to save the extra $250 we charged for general anesthesia, so she was awake at the start of the abortion. Unfortunately, she looked down during the procedure and saw the baby's hand as the doctor took it out.

I heard her gasp, saw what she saw, and quickly covered her eyes, but I was too late. She had already passed out.

When she came to, the doctor was finished. The young woman looked up at me with horror in her eyes and asked me about what she had seen.

"I don't know what you're talking about," I lied.

"But I saw a part of my baby! I know I did!"

"Honey, I was there the whole time, and I didn't see a thing. You must have imagined it."

If you think it was hard maintaining my composure in such situations, you're right. Believe me, it takes a lot of beers to make yourself forget what you're doing.

Two weeks later, when this young woman returned for her follow-up exam, she looked at me accusingly. The first thing she said was, "You know what I saw. You *know.*" The sweetness in her spirit had died; there was now a hard edge to her voice.

I avoided her eyes for fear I'd give it all away.

A Hundred-Dollar Lie

That was not the only lie I was expected to tell. More than once I had a conversation with Arnie that went something like this.

"She's ten weeks, Arnie."

"Norma, tell her she's twelve."

I tried looking him in the eye, but he avoided my stare. The difference between an abortion at ten weeks and twelve weeks was a hundred dollars. Abortionists routinely jack up the estimate of a baby's age because most women simply won't argue about it—and even fewer would dare to solicit a second, more informed opinion.

In this arena, the abortionist is freer than any other physician. He controls both the sonogram and the sonogram machine, and rarely has to confer with another doctor or share his records. Since he is talking to women who are almost universally uninformed about the mechanics of what he does, it is child's play to cash in by inflating an unborn baby's age.

"You tell her," I said. "I'm not gonna lie."

I was not always cooperative. For example, both Connie and I refused to reassemble the body parts after a late-term abortion. It was bad enough having to seal the bags that held them, but there was no way I was going to treat those bodies like grotesque jigsaw puzzles.

"Norma, Norma," Arnie once told me, "I will show you where to put the tissue."

Tissue was the code word for *bodies* in our clinic. We stored them in plastic bags, which were kept in a freezer until they were picked up weekly.

I was not a newcomer to abortion clinics at that time, but I was not about to handle the bodies. "Sorry, Arnie," I said, "I don't do that. I'll scrub the floors. I'll make appointments. But don't ask me to handle the tissue."

"Is okay," he argued. "I show you how to put in freezer."

I walked in the back, more to shut up Arnie than to commit to handling the bodies in the future. Besides, I was feeling a little ashamed of myself.

You're hard-core, I told myself. *You're Jane Roe. You can handle a couple of plastic bags full of tissue.*

The Parts Room, as we called it, was narrow, with washbasins on one side and medical supplies on the other. Against one wall was a white freezer with the lock broken off.

Arnie lifted up a large plastic bag. The contents looked similar to a cut-up chicken, with all the parts swimming in blood, and I felt myself grow nauseous. Then I saw the back of a head float by and I immediately vomited all over Arnie, the sink, and the counter.

"Oh, Norma," Arnie complained, "I will have to go and clean myself again." He looked at me and sighed.

"You cannot do this?" he asked.

I was white. I thought I might throw up again. And he was asking me if I was sure I couldn't do this?

I shook my head. "No."

"This is okay," he answered. "I will have Connie do it."

Connie also refused, so Arnie ended up piecing the bodies together himself. At the beginning of each week, a service truck would come by and pick up the body parts, which were taken to a lab.

All through the week, the Parts Room became creepier and creepier. I never wanted to go back there, especially at night. Sometimes I had to go back there to fix the phone lines or get some supplies, and every time I would be afraid that the freezer was going to open, reach out and grab me, and pull me into its cold world, slamming shut.

No, I was not losing my mind; but when you work at an abortion clinic, you're guilty and you know it. For all the millions spent on public relations, the abortion movement has yet to invent rhetoric powerful enough to blind abortion clinic workers from the truth. You see the body parts, you hear the women's cries, and you can't keep lying to yourself—at least not without artificial stimulation.

That's why drugs, alcohol, and coarse jokes are so popular inside the clinics. If we had stayed sober and not laughed at ourselves, we would have begun to think of ourselves as hideous monsters preying on little babies.

CHAPTER 10

"Thanks, but No Thanks"

Do you see anything?"

"No. What about you?"

"It looks clear to me."

Connie and I looked at each other. "Run!" We got out of the truck, rushed into the clinic, then slammed the door shut behind us, locking it as quickly as possible.

We had survived our first morning of showing up for work with Operation Rescue as a next-door neighbor.

When news first filtered out that O.R. had secured the office suite next to ours, we and most of the proabortion movement assumed that Flip Benham had outdone himself in staging such a coup. Their opportunities to protest and harass us would increase immeasurably, and we naturally assumed this was all part of Flip's strategy.

But as smart as Flip was, he actually did everything he could to *avoid* moving next door to us. The story of O.R.'s relocation is not one of intrigue, plotting, or back-room strategizing—at least not from a human perspective. If anybody was strategizing, it was the angels.

Here's the story.

In January 1995, Flip Benham received a phone call from a real estate agent named Clark Skaggs. "Flip," Clark began, "I've got this place; it's right next door to an abortion mill, *but-the-abortion-mill-is-moving-out.*" Clark said this last part as quickly as possible because he knew it would be a deal breaker as far as Flip was concerned.

Flip sighed. Rescue was looking for new offices, but there was no particular rush, and he didn't want to be near an abortion clinic for even a short time.

"Thanks," he said, "but no thanks."

Clark was persistent—so persistent, in fact, that he even visited Flip's church to present the idea a second time. As he introduced Flip to his wife, he said, "By the way, she agrees with me that it would be a wonderful thing if you moved right next door to the mill. This abortion mill has to move out because the landlord's insurance rates are going up over 300 percent as long as the mill stays."

When Flip broached the idea with his assistant, Ronda Mackey, she was cautious. Ronda could not fathom trying to carry on a ministry right next door to an abortion clinic. But within days O.R. found out that their current office building had been sold to a new owner, who would not renew their lease. In fact, their lease would end in less than a month, so overnight the important became urgent—they had to find a new place to stay, and Clark was certain he had found the right place.

Ronda agreed to meet with Clark, but when she saw the building, she was anything but pleased with it. The complex looked completely run-down. Clark showed Ronda three different suites, but the only one that would work was the suite that shared a wall with A Choice for Women. To make matters worse, the available space was smoky and in need of a good cleaning. There weren't any windows, the carpet was dark, the paneling was dark, and it smelled.

Ronda politely told Clark that O.R. would keep looking and then found another office that seemed much better. As far as Ronda was concerned, the more she thought about it, the more she realized there was no comparison, so she set up an appointment to sign the lease at the other property.

The morning of that appointment, however, Ronda received one last call from Clark. "Ronda," Clark said, "God is orchestrating this, I just know it. You've got to give this office one more chance. You can sign the other lease tomorrow. It won't hurt to meet with the landlord of this other building first, will it? He really wants to meet you, and he's prepared to give you a great deal."

Ronda had her mind made up, but she's the type of woman who is always willing to explore the possibility that God might be orchestrating something else. She agreed to meet the landlord and set up a meeting with another O.R. volunteer named Rick Blinn. The landlord presented himself to Ronda and Rick as a Christian businessman, and they were immediately taken in by his kindness.

"What does your group do?" he asked.

"We help women in crisis pregnancies."

"Oh—you help battered women?"

"No, we help women in crisis pregnancies."

"Well, I lease to a battered women's center upstairs. Good people."

Because controversy clings to O.R. like mud clings to a dog, Ronda knew that an amiable landlord could be even more important than a favorable office. She began to change her mind about the other lease, but there was one thing she had to get out of the way right up front.

"If we decide to move in here, we want it in the lease that the abortion clinic will move out. We do not want to operate our ministry next door to an abortion mill."

The landlord smiled. "Give me two weeks, and I'll have them out of there," he said, then paused. "No, better give me four weeks. I don't want to get in a lawsuit."

Ronda was amazed. Maybe God really was orchestrating this. After all, not only could they secure a sympathetic landlord, but they could indirectly cause an abortion clinic to lose its lease and be forced to find a new home. Women would come to sign up for an abortion, but nothing would be there—except a crisis pregnancy center!

This sounded almost too good to be true, so Ronda and Rick reported back to Flip, and the decision was made that they would move in next door.

We were not told any of this at A Choice for Women. In fact, since the offices on each side of us were vacant, we had planned to expand. The landlord never told us we would have to be out in four years, much less four weeks. The only notification we got about O.R.'s lease was when they started moving in.

Free Rent

Meanwhile, Operation Rescue was getting ready for a quick move. They had less than two days left on their current lease, so they would have to move fast. As they started packing, Flip received a phone call from Clark.

"Flip, I've got some bad news. We reread the lease, and it says the abortion mill does not have to move until June of 1996." Originally Flip had agreed that A Choice for Women could stay until June of 1995. He sighed. O.R. had nowhere else to go. In two days they would be out on the street. But did he really want to work next door to an abortion clinic for over a year?

"Listen," Clark continued, "I've talked to the landlord and he said he'll give you that space rent-free if you agree to stay until the abortion mill moves out."

Flip smiled. Not only would the abortion clinic be forced to move out, but O.R. would get over a year's free rent. Maybe this wasn't such a bad deal after all!

"It gets even better," Clark added. "For a dollar a month, he'll give us the option to lease the space occupied by the abortion clinic once they move out."

What was really going on was that the landlord feared a lawsuit—and for good reason. A Choice for Women would definitely have fought him if he had tried to evict us. He never intended to force us out, but he hoped that by inviting O.R. next door, we would become so miserable we would leave of our own accord—and his insurance rates would go back down. And apparently he had run the figures and discovered that because of his insurance rates, it would be cheaper to give the space away than to rent it to us.

Operation Rescue did their best to keep the lease a secret for as long as possible. They feared a massive demonstration if word leaked out, so Ronda came over with just a few women and quietly slipped inside the front door, hoping to clean up the place a bit before Flip and the men began packing in the boxes. We never heard any of the cleaning; they caught us totally off guard.

But they were caught off guard as well. Flip and Ronda knew it would be controversial for O.R. to move next door to an abortion clinic, but they had no idea they were moving next door to Jane Roe's abortion clinic; Flip thought I was still working at the abortion clinic across town. If they had known I was there, I'm not sure they would have moved in.

So it was a big surprise on all sides. For our part, on one day, we were making plans to occupy the space next door. The next thing we knew, Flip Venom was pulling up in a big Ryder truck.

That's the day, you'll recall, that I opted to drink my lunch.

CHAPTER 11

Circus 'R' Us

If you were to go back to 1995 and look at the Dallas police blotter, you would see that traveling to A Choice for Women and the new offices of Operation Rescue was more than a daily occurrence for the average police officer. It was practically an hourly one. Several times a day the familiar "bleep, bleep" of the police car sirens and the flashing blue lights would be right outside our clinic doors.

The Rescue people proved more resilient than cockroaches. We simply could not scare them off. We couldn't humiliate them. We couldn't get them to leave. Abortions were performed Thursday through Saturday, so the tensions inevitably increased to a fevered pitch during those days.

With O.R. next door, we reevaluated our floor plan and decided to move my office away from the common wall with O.R. to the other side of the suite. I was often on the phone, setting up appointments, and we did not want O.R. to be able to listen in. We could hear them talking through the wall if we tried, so we knew they could hear us as well.

From the receptionist's office, I could see Ronda talking to women right outside our front window as they made their way into my clinic, and it made me furious. When I saw one woman start to turn around, I charged out the front door.

"It's none of your business, leave her alone!" I yelled out, waving my arms around like I was swatting flies. "Get out of her face!"

Over the years, I had learned that my temper could be a potent weapon. People melted in the face of it. They expected women to be weak or frail or polite, and when they saw me charging out like a bull, the surprise factor alone was usually enough to make them back down. That was not the case with Ronda. Though she's very attractive, with a petite build, she's street tough. You underestimate Ronda at your own peril.

The client turned back around and joined me to go into the abortion clinic.

Ronda sighed, then turned around to leave.

"Good day, Ronda," I added sarcastically as she walked off.

"After that baby is dead, your day is not going to be so good," Ronda called back.

"Save it for somebody else, Ronda," I said. "It's her decision."

The next day, Friday, a woman and her granddaughter came into the clinic. Before we could do anything, we had to get a sonogram to determine how far along the pregnancy was.

"It'll cost you a hundred dollars for the sonogram," I told the grandmother.

"I want to pay for it all now," she said.

"We can't do that," I explained. "We don't know how much to charge you until we know how far along your granddaughter is. You have to pay for the sonogram in advance, and then afterward we'll know what to charge you for the abortion."

"I don't want to do it that way," she insisted. "I just want to pay one time."

Friday mornings were busy. We were doing procedures and I did not feel like arguing. "Then you'll just have to wait," I said.

"But—" She started talking like she was going to change her mind, but I wasn't about to play games with her.

"Come back in an hour," I said.

She went back out the door and sat in her car with her granddaughter. I knew she was an out-of-towner and had no place to go, so I was not surprised that she stayed in her car. That had never been a problem before, but then, Rescue had never been a next-door neighbor before, either.

When Flip came to work that morning, he saw the woman and her granddaughter sitting in the car, and he went up and started talking to them. Of course, they didn't have a clue about who he was. He found out they were there to get a sonogram and an abortion, and Flip started sharing his testimony and the gospel.

The Most Selfish Man Who Ever Lived

Though today Flip works for a substandard wage, lives in a very modest home, and spends the best hours of his days on behalf of the unborn, by his own admission he was, at one point in his life, the most selfish man who ever lived.

Flip was born and raised in the saloon business. When he was twenty-seven years old, he owned the Mad Hatter Saloon in Kissimmee, Florida. In Flip's words, he was a "total drunk with a lot of money—the most dangerous kind of alcoholic you can be."

The story of my conversion is full of ironies, and one of the most surprising is that when Flip's wife, Faye, became pregnant early on in their marriage, Flip urged her to get an abortion. "I was surrounded north, south, east, and west by me," he explains. "I just didn't have room in my heart for anyone else."

Faye refused. "You have no choice," she told him. "We're going to have this baby." It's not easy standing up to Flip, but Faye remained firm, and today, Flip loves her for it. It turned out that Faye was actually pregnant with twin boys, who today are Flip's best friends.

A guy who sold coffeemakers came into Flip's saloon on a sales call and started talking about Jesus Christ, but at first, Flip didn't sense the need. Though he did not go to church, he considered himself a Christian already. *After all,* he thought, *I'm not a Buddhist or a Muslim. What else could I be?*

Flip's saloon was full of hypocrites who went to church every Sunday but drank themselves into oblivion at his bar Monday through Saturday; he didn't see any difference in the way they lived and the way he lived, except for how they spent those few hours on Sunday mornings.

"I knew I wasn't an A or even a B person, morally," Flip explains, "but I also figured I wasn't a D or an F person—I didn't rob, rape, or kill anybody. What it came down to was that I was about average—a C person—and I just assumed that C persons and above got into heaven."

In spite of this, Flip sensed that he was out of control. He stayed loaded as much as he could, and fought off a recurring dream of being on a bar stool, falling back, and flinging his arms to keep his balance.

More out of politeness than anything else, Flip agreed to go to church with the coffeemaker salesman. He never expected the man to actually show up on Sunday morning (Flip's house was attached to the saloon), so he was astonished when he heard the doorbell ring.

"Are you ready?" the salesman asked.

"No," Flip admitted, "I'm not."

Since the man had taken the trouble to show up, Flip felt he owed it to him to get ready, so he and his wife got the kids as presentable as possible in a hurry and went to church for the first time ever as a family.

The church was a small Free Methodist congregation, full of wintering snowbirds. The pastor preached the gospel with conviction and compassion, and Flip's heart was torn in two.

After the service, Flip told Faye to drive the kids home; he wanted to walk. With each step, Flip cried fresh tears of repentance, cut to the heart by the gospel message. After a few minutes, he could hardly walk, stumbling along the side of the road.

He looked like he was drunk, but he had never been more sober in his life.

Flip went back the next Sunday, and the Sunday after that, and the Sunday after that. Still wary of the hypocrites who frequented his tavern, he wanted to see if this Christianity was real. Soon he found himself going back to church on Sunday nights.

One day Flip caught himself humming a gospel tune as he stocked the saloon's coolers. *Am I turning into a fruitcake?* he wondered. He was afraid that if he took his faith seriously, he'd become like the guy who dragged a cross from Daytona to Tampa and back, always stopping in front of Flip's saloon to call out the Lord's judgments.

"God, please don't make me a fruitcake for you," Flip pleaded. But during the day, he couldn't stay away from the Bible, so he read it between pouring drinks at the saloon.

Then he got the crazy idea of enrolling in a tiny Bible college in Lake Wales. Flip began closing the saloon at 3 A.M. and waking up at 6 A.M. to catch an 8 A.M. class. He was like a sponge, soaking up the Bible from Genesis to Revelation.

Soon people at the saloon started asking Flip, "What's the matter with you? You've changed." Flip's professors also noticed a change, and one of them suggested that Flip go to seminary.

"But I can't," Flip protested. "I'm already married."

Flip thought a seminary and a monastery were the same thing! Once the professor set him straight, Flip sent in an application, found himself accepted, and put the saloon up for sale.

He never looked back.

Flip graduated from seminary in 1980 and then started and pastored a church in Dallas, Texas. At this point, he was still pro-choice. Flip never questioned the morality of abortion until he went to a Bill Gothard seminar in 1982. Gothard taught out of Philippians 2, explaining that when the Holy Spirit came upon Mary and conception occurred, God was there, in the flesh, at that moment.

In 1984 Flip became involved with Last Harvest Ministries and helped set up a crisis pregnancy center and maternity home.

He was at the Democratic National Convention in 1988 when he saw a "little old lady," a Baptist Sunday school teacher, handcuffed and thrown into a police truck for lying down in front of an abortion clinic.

We have the same theology, Flip thought to himself, *but she's living it out while I'm not.* Flip knew what jail was like—he had been arrested for driving while intoxicated—so he was reluctant to get involved with the new movement called Operation Rescue. Even so, he felt humiliated when he compared his own faith to that of the elderly Sunday school teacher.

Over time, God broke down Flip's reluctance, and he eventually participated in his first rescue. In 1992 he spent time in jail with Randall Terry (O.R.'s founder) and Keith Tucci (O.R.'s second director). When Randall stepped down as O.R.'s leader, and Keith Tucci followed suit a few years later, Flip was asked to take over.

"Norma, We Just Had Our First Save!"

After Flip finished sharing his testimony with the woman and her granddaughter, he invited them into Rescue's office. A counselor, Jessie Ann, took over from there. By the time Jessie Ann got through with them, there was no way that baby was going to be aborted. The woman thanked the O.R. volunteers and left without saying a word to me.

When I came outside to smoke a cigarette with some of the other clinic workers, I saw that the grandmother's car was gone, but I assumed they must have driven to a McDonald's or something. A few minutes later, Ronda walked by and yelled out, "Norma, we just had our first save! A mama just chose life for her baby! Aren't you happy?"

I put two and two together and realized whom she was talking about, and something erupted inside me. I don't know what it was. To be honest, it did not take much to set me off in those days. I flew off the bench I had been sitting on, charged Ronda, and showered her with expletives and spittle until two clinic workers pulled me back. They had seen my temper before, but this outburst scared them.

"Norma," they said, "let it go."

But I was as angry as I had ever been. I was used to doing business my way, and that meant I didn't have to take any guff from the patients. Rescue was changing everything. I apparently could not leave a patient alone for more than five minutes without having Rescue pluck her out of our hands, and I didn't like the competition. I was good at getting people into the clinic, and I was excellent at having them show up for appointments. I had a record and a reputation to protect, and Ronda was taking that away.

I felt some satisfaction as I watched Ronda hurry away, but once she was out of sight, I realized that the momentum in the abortion debate in Dallas had shifted yet again. For several years, the practice of rescuing had turned providing abortions into a messy business. It could take hours to open a clinic on Saturday mornings if O.R. showed up, and often clients would take one look at the circus and drive away, some of them never coming back.

The proabortion movement had fought back by getting the Freedom to Access Clinic Entrances (FACE) Act passed, and this all but shut Rescue down. We managed to convince the legislators that a person sitting down in front of an abortion clinic should be liable for a $100,000 fine and a year in jail—for a first offense! Normally, trespass resulted in a waived fine, a warning, and that was about it. But when some angry feminists got involved, trespassing suddenly became a felony—provided it was done in front of an abortion clinic.

When FACE was passed, we knew we had won. Even the most dedicated of pro-lifers could not justify such outrageous penalties. Large-scale rescues plummeted to near zero. Finally, we were allowed to perform our business in relative quiet.

But that day, as Ronda cast a worried glance behind her, making sure the clinic workers were still holding me back, I realized that the calm, rather peaceful life that we had enjoyed at the clinic for a year or so had come to an end. It was war all over again, but that was okay by me. Norma McCorvey was not afraid of any war.

I would fight it to the bitter end.

CHAPTER 12

God and Goddess Talk

Though I was ready for war with Rescue, I was not ready for Rescue's weapons. This would not be a war of trying to outsmart demonstrators. This was not a war about who could come up with the best slogans, or who could gather the largest crowds. I was ready for that war, but that was not the war we fought.

The war that went on in front of our clinic became a war of love and hatred. I threw out every expletive I could imagine, and the Rescue people threw back affirmations. They never backed down from calling what I was doing sin, but while they showed a rock-hard opposition to everything I stood for, at the same time they displayed an incredible openness to reach out to me as a person.

It wasn't long before Flip was talking to me about God, and I was talking to him about the goddess.

"Miss Norma, What Are We Going to Do?"

The first Saturday after Rescue moved in, I was again having a cigarette, sitting on a bench in front of the clinic, and enjoying what had turned out to be a stunningly beautiful day. The sun was out, the sky was a piercing blue, but it wasn't so hot that you couldn't enjoy it. The temperature was just right.

It can't get much better than this, I was thinking to myself, when Flip walked over and stood in front of me, blocking my sun.

"Miss Norma," he said, "I'm going to talk to about ten post-abortive women later today and help them come to grips with what they've done and how they can be healed. Want to come along?"

I snorted. "I don't think so," I said, loading my voice with sarcasm.

Flip smiled and then asked if he could join me on the bench.

"It's a free country."

Flip sat down—finally, I had my sun back—and looked at me. "Miss Norma, Miss Norma," he said, "what are we going to do?"

I shrugged my shoulders. I didn't have a clue.

"Can I talk with you for a minute?" he asked.

"Well, sure."

"I have wanted to apologize to you for what happened at the book signing a few months back. I saw my words drop into your heart, and I know they hurt you deeply. I'm sorry. Will you forgive me?"

Flip could have turned purple on the spot, and it would not have surprised me any more than hearing him say, "I'm sorry." Men had been jerks to me all my life. I thought that was the way all men were, so it didn't surprise me when Flip turned out to be a jerk. But a man who apologized for it? A man who said he was sorry?

Was this guy for real?

I immediately excused myself, went back into my office, and cried. I was furious at Flip, and at the same time I liked him. It was really strange, carrying such conflicting emotions, and it further confused me. I thought back just a few days, to the afternoon when Flip and O.R. had moved in next door. I remembered the way he had suddenly seemed so human. Now he also seemed to be sensitive and caring.

What was going on? How could I fight this?

"But the Goddess Puts It This Way . . ."

Flip's apology was the most potent assault I had ever known. I was defenseless against it. Now that the wall between us had been demolished, Flip and I began talking on almost a daily basis. He explained why he had become a Christian, and then shared why he was led to apologize to me.

"Miss Norma," he said, "the Bible says in Romans 7:14–17, 'For we know that the law is spiritual, but I am carnal, sold under sin. For what I am doing, I do not understand. For what I will to do, that I do not practice; but what I hate, that I do. If, then, I do what I will not to do, I agree with the law that it is good. But now, it is no longer I who do it, but sin that dwells in me.'

"You see, Miss Norma, that's the part of me that yelled at you at the book signing. That's why I told you I'm simply a great big sinner saved by a great big God."

Flip took me through Romans 7:23–25: "But I see another law in my members, warring against the law of my mind, and bringing me into captivity to the law of sin which is in my members. O wretched man that I am! Who will deliver me from this body of death? I thank God—through Jesus Christ our Lord! So then, with the mind I myself serve the law of God, but with the flesh the law of sin."

I could not pretend that at times I didn't feel wretched too. I thought of my drunken binges and the occasional forays into cocaine and the not-so-infrequent outbursts of anger. Certainly, something wretched was going on inside of me, but I wasn't at all sure that, like Paul, I needed to turn to Jesus. I had other ways of seeking spiritual guidance.

"I've listened to you," I told Flip on a later occasion, "now you have to listen to me."

"All right, Miss Norma, I'm listening."

I was raised a Jehovah's Witness Roman Catholic (yeah, I know, those two don't normally go together, but that's my family). Over the years I added a little American Indian religion, New Age practices, and just about anything else that seemed a little mystical. Flip was about to get a taste of my religious smorgasbord.

I took out my Book of Runes with my little stone tablets engraved with Egyptian hieroglyphics. You shake them in a bag and then throw them out. The way the stones land is supposed to be an indicator of how your day will go: "breakthrough," "partnership," or "protection." Flip watched me do my thing and smiled, then talked some more about how God orders our paths.

I wouldn't give an inch. "But the goddess doesn't work that way," I argued, always making the deity feminine.

Flip was patient, but persistent. He did not ridicule my beliefs, but he never affirmed them, either, instead patiently explaining the Christian perspective.

All of this took place on that bench outdoors. But soon, I'd become a frequent visitor to O.R.'s office.

Bumps on the Wall

The first time I actually walked into Rescue's offices, I was madder than a hornet. We were trying to get some business done, and they were banging away on the walls like crazy. I'm not the type of person who will go all day with a rock in her shoe rather than stop to take it out. If I'm uncomfortable, I'm gonna do something about it, so I already had it in mind to say something when Arnie came into my office, whiter than the sheet of paper I was shuffling across my desk.

"That noise," he gasped. "What do you think it is?"

"If it's a bomb, I'd say it's a pretty big one," I teased him.

"Miss Norma," he said, trying to look as professional as possible in his bare feet, "you must do something, you must stop that. I can't counsel girls."

I charged into Rescue's offices. It never occurred to me to knock, which was probably for the best. Considering the state I was in, I might have broken the door down in the process. Ronda looked over at me, completely startled. O.R. had their space and we had ours, and there was an unwritten rule that that space could never, ever, be violated. Yet here I was, shaking my finger in their faces—in their suite!

"Look, you guys," I shouted, "what's going on here? What's all this banging about?"

As soon as I shouted the words, I saw Rene (another O.R. volunteer) with a hammer in his hand, which he dropped quickly to his side. There was an awkward pause as I realized they were not trying to be obnoxious; they were simply hanging up their posters, certificates, and banners. I felt kind of silly, but I'm not the type of person who backpedals so I said, "Why don't you do this on Sunday or something? We're trying to run a clinic."

For good measure, I added, "How can we kill babies with all this racket going on?"

Ronda and Rene didn't say a word. They were just astonished that I had the nerve to walk right in without knocking. Of course, if they did that in our offices, the police would arrest them, and they would wind up in jail, a national top-of-the-hour news story for sure.

But there's a deeper story to my charge into Rescue's offices. When O.R. first moved in, I had told the media that we naturally feared for our safety. "The vultures will terrorize us if we turn our backs for a minute," I warned.

Now, instinctively, I realized that they wouldn't hurt me. Whatever this banging was all about, somehow I knew it wasn't a threat. We might be on opposite sides of the abortion issue, but my life was not in danger, even if I charged into their offices uninvited.

Another stereotype had fallen.

New Water

"Get a load of this," Connie said. I took the letter from her hand and read it. The landlord was practically doubling our rent, citing "substantially increased annual premiums" from the insurance company.

"I think he's trying to get rid of us," I said. Of course, neither Connie nor I knew at the time that this was part of his calculated effort to remove us from the building, in accordance with his agreement with O.R.

"Raising our rent by thirty-five thousand dollars a year is a good way to do it." Connie laughed.

"We won't let them win," I insisted. "We won't let them win."

In spite of my tough words, something about the atmosphere next door was inviting to me. My visits to the Rescue offices became regular. To my coworkers at the clinic, I made it seem like a game. "I'm gonna go see what the *Christians* are doing today." But inside I looked forward to my visits.

Sometimes I'd be in a rotten mood, cussing and swearing and talking everyone and everything down. "Y'all are vultures," I'd say, "stealing my clients!" Other times, I'd be like a pleasant next-door neighbor. They saw me at my best, and they saw me at my worst. At the time, I was a victim of my own moods. I didn't have the power to overcome the mood swings, so the O.R. people saw me just as I was—but they never pulled away. If I had chewed them out during a bad mood and went back the next day, I was never chastised for the way I had treated them the day before. They simply said, "Hi, Miss Norma, what's up?"

The way they treated me almost bothered me, as if they knew something I didn't. But what could that something be? What did they have up their sleeves?

I became a self-appointed detective, determined to figure out what made these people tick. I watched Flip drive up, then get out of the car, that big Bible invariably tucked under his arm. He seemed to always be in such a good mood (I've since discovered that I was very wrong on this last observation!). And then Ronda would drive up in her minivan with her two children, always smiling and looking fresh and pretty and finding a way to be pleasant.

The other O.R. volunteers would come in, and I'd never see them frown. I looked behind me, at the people working in the clinic, and noticed that I rarely saw anyone smile, especially in the morning.

These Christians must be taking some powerful kind of drugs! I said to myself. *Nobody can be that happy.*

I fought against the thought that their happiness might have something to do with this "God" that Flip kept talking about. I even tried to talk myself out of liking them. When I saw one of them drive up I'd say to Connie, "Well, here come the zealots. I guess we're going to be Christianized again today."

But they never shoved anything down my throat. They simply passed along a cup of refreshing spiritual water, confident that I was thirsty and that I would take a drink whenever I was in a mood where I could receive it—which I occasionally did.

They didn't warn me about how potent that water could be.

CHAPTER

13 Baby Malachi

In spite of the occasional personal goodwill between us, there was still a great deal of professional animosity. As marketing director for A Choice for Women, I had my hands full. I was supposed to sell abortions—we didn't make a dime on an appointment, only on an actual procedure—so I had to overcome all the O.R. paraphernalia that now gathered outside our front door.

With Operation Rescue came Rescue families, and that meant baby buggies, strollers, and little kids—not exactly the type of image an abortion clinic wants to present to its clients. How could we convince a young mother to abort her child when she drives up and finds children laughing and playing right next door?

But the worst was when the Rescue people started displaying a giant photograph of Baby Malachi. How this poster came to be is a story in itself.

In April 1993 Ronda was struggling with her role as an Operation Rescue volunteer. Many of her Christian friends had begun to back away from her. This hurt Ronda, and caused her to reconsider what she was doing. It was impossible not to reconsider it when she was so frequently challenged.

"What you're doing isn't right!"

"How can you block doors? That's violent!"

"Don't you think trespassing is a little bit fanatical?"

"Christians shouldn't break the law, ever!"

Ronda was in charge of the sidewalk counselors who worked side by side with the rescuers at their demonstrations. While the rescuers blocked the door, sidewalk counselors would approach clients, hand them some literature, and try to engage them in conversation, hoping to dissuade them from having an abortion.

On one particular morning, Ronda led her counselors *inside* the clinic to talk to the women in the waiting room of the North Dallas Women's Clinic. The police usually gave warnings, so Ronda intended to lead her counselors out as soon as the police asked them to leave. That way, none of the counselors would be arrested.

That's the way it was supposed to work, anyway. Yet there was always a chance that they might draw a police officer who didn't believe in warnings. In that case, the counselors would be arrested on the spot; but Ronda was willing to risk that.

O.R. had arrived before most of the clients had. The clinic director was there, as was a local abortion advocate, and just two clients. Immediately, the director began shuttling the two clients into separate rooms, trying to keep them away from the counselors. Ronda did not want to smother the two clients, so she let two counselors follow the clients while she took advantage of the diversion and managed to slip into the back of the clinic.

Ronda opened the door to the first room where abortions were actually performed, and as she states it, she ran into a "spiritual wall." The door was opened, but she couldn't push through; something unseen was holding her back.

The sight alone made her sick to her stomach. She saw dried blood on the legs of the table. It was so filthy that she felt nauseous.

Unable to enter, Ronda shut the door and prayed, "God, please let me find the babies." She knew there had to be a room where the clinic kept the aborted children, and Ronda wanted to find it. If she actually saw the babies, she thought, that would be enough to resolve her confusion about why she was willing to sacrifice so much of her time to work with Operation Rescue.

Ronda knew the police were coming and that speed was critical, and she was determined to make the best use of every single second. "Please, God," she prayed, "if this is really what you want us to be doing, I want to see a sign. I want to see the babies and witness firsthand what the abortion clinic is doing."

Ronda felt led to go into the lab room, but a rescuer grabbed her arm. "We've already been in there," he said. "We didn't find anything."

Ronda said, "Thanks," but for some reason, decided not to turn around. She looked over in the middle of the room and saw a big white freezer. Her heart started beating a little bit faster as she slowly walked up to it. Ronda touched the lid, felt a chill, and opened it.

It was full of jars, dozens of them, every one full of tiny body parts. Ronda gasped as she saw minuscule hands and feet pressing against the sides of the jars, frozen in a mixture of blood.

"I found the babies!" she gasped. "I found them!"

She ran out of the room and saw some of the rescuers who were blocking the procedure room. "I found the babies! I found the babies! What do I do?"

"Get the camera!" someone yelled. "Get the camera!"

Rescuers always appointed someone to take a videotape of the rescue. For all the rhetoric we proabortion people spewed about the "violent rescues," the truth is, the police officers and clinic personnel perpetrated most of the violence. The rescuers always stayed passive and limp; for this, some of them were rewarded with broken arms, sprayed with mace, and worse. The rescuers finally wised up and began bringing video cameras onsite because nobody would believe them. "You're the ones breaking the law," people protested, "not the police officers."

The guy with the camera at this rescue was relatively small, about five feet five, but he eagerly climbed over the rescuers and followed Ronda into the lab. "Look," Ronda pointed out, "you can see the hands and feet, and here's a leg!"

The guy with the camera took one look at the jars, fell to his knees, and started bawling. He couldn't take it. It was the most grotesque and inhumane thing he had ever seen, and the grisliness overpowered him.

"Get up," Ronda yelled at him. "You've got to get up! The police are coming, and we have to get this on tape or people will never believe us!"

Finally, the cameraman stood up, aimed his camera, and began filming the jars in the freezer.

Other rescuers started filing in, when someone pointed out, "The police will be here any minute. Someone needs to take a jar out."

"I can't do it," Ronda said. The jars were so full that when the lids were closed, blood had run over and was frozen to the outside. Clearly, each jar held more than one child. Ronda was wearing a white sweatsuit and was afraid that if she tucked the jar under her jacket, the blood frozen on the outside of the jar would begin to melt and seep right through her clothing. Besides, she would never be able to get the jar out of the clinic without being noticed.

A woman with a heavier winter coat came in, and she agreed to slip a jar underneath it. Surrounded by Ronda and a few other rescuers, the woman casually walked out with the jar.

Operation Rescue set up an appointment with a sympathetic pro-life doctor who agreed to help them unfreeze the jar and examine the contents. The doctor opened the jar and took out the remains and pieces of four very small children, but the jar was still two-thirds full.

"Oh my," he said.

"What?" Ronda asked. "What's wrong?"

Just then a nurse came in. "Doctor, you've got an urgent call."

The doctor looked at Ronda and the others. "Sorry," he said, and ran out. He did not come back for several hours, and Ronda kept wondering what he had meant by, "Oh my."

When the doctor came back, he looked grim. "Had to deliver a baby," he explained.

"What was the 'Oh my' all about?" Ronda asked.

The doctor said, "This is a big one." He then pulled out a severed head, a torso, and two legs.

"It was a boy," he said. The doctor estimated he was about twenty-one weeks old.

Normally, Ronda has a very weak stomach, but she was so moved with pity for this child, she could actually hold him and feel empathy rather than disgust. Even though his entrails were hanging out, and his ear was partially torn off (the work of the forceps, the doctor explained), he looked beautiful to Ronda.

Later that day, Ronda called Flip, told him about their discovery, and said, "I want to name him Baby Malachi. I always wanted a boy, and I thought I would name him Malachi."

Flip paused. "You need a better reason than that. Go through the Bible and find a reason why you think we should name this boy Malachi, and we'll go with that."

Ronda consulted her study Bible, where she learned that *Malachi* means "God's messenger." *What better role for this boy than to be God's messenger?* she thought. Malachi could open up people's eyes to the truth about abortion.

And then, as she read through the book of Malachi and came to the very end, she found her verse: "And he will turn / The hearts of the fathers to the children, / And the hearts of the children to their fathers, / Lest I come and strike the earth with a curse" (4:6).

"When people see this baby's picture," Ronda explained to Flip, "he's going to turn the fathers' hearts back to the plight of their children. He's going to be able to speak to them in a way we can't. He's going to be God's messenger."

Flip readily consented, and the aborted boy had his name.

Malachi was buried along with the other four children who had been kept in that jar, but not until Operation Rescue had taken a picture, which showed in stark detail the results of abortion. This picture, which they had blown up into a poster, became my biggest headache as marketing director for our abortion clinic. However much we tried to convince the women that they weren't really aborting a baby, Malachi showed them otherwise. The old saying, "A picture is worth a thousand words," was doubly true when it came to that poster. We made a living out of telling women they were simply doing away with a "blob of tissue," a "product of conception," or even a "missed menstrual period"—as if you could abort a period!

Baby Malachi was impossible to overcome, so I made a deal with O.R. "Tell you what," I told Ronda. "You keep that Baby Malachi poster out of here and I'll let you have three minutes with every client."

I was so confident of our clinic's ability to keep the women who came in, I felt certain O.R.'s three minutes would be meaningless. They couldn't possibly change their minds, I thought. I was wrong, of course, but I didn't know that then. I just wanted Baby Malachi out of there.

Ronda knew a good deal when she saw it. She would much rather have three minutes with a client than be able to display a single poster, so she readily agreed; Baby Malachi came down.

I had my biggest hurdle out of the way. The second major hurdle—the playing children—was more difficult to overcome, in part because I gained a mother's love for one of them in particular.

She was Ronda's daughter, and her name was Emily.

CHAPTER 14

A Girl Named Emily

One of the brightest young Rescue girls who played outside our front door was Emily, Ronda Mackey's then seven-year-old daughter. She is a petite little girl, with brown hair, green eyes, and a little wrinkle in her nose that pops up whenever she smiles. God got hold of Emily early. Even at the age of seven she was a little evangelist with a heart full of love.

Since we were literally next-door neighbors to O.R., we shared a common sidewalk. Ronda spent so much time volunteering for Rescue that her two children, Emily and Chelsey, would frequently play outside. As kids naturally do, Emily and Chelsey claimed the entire sidewalk. There were no boundaries for them. They were two little girls at play, and it made no difference whether their play space was closer to the clinic than to Rescue's offices.

One morning I was out having a cigarette and watching Chelsey and Emily playing ring-around-a-rosy right in front of our clinic doors. The two girls started skipping past the awning that was over our front door.

I watched them and thought, *Oh, that's so sweet.*

A clinic escort was also out smoking a cigarette. She watched the children play, but as she did so, an increasingly ugly expression took over her face. It was as if she took the little girls' laughter personally. Finally, she stuck out her foot to trip them.

I threw my cigarette down and yelled at her. "Say, ma'am, aren't you a bit old to play games like that? They're little kids, just playing games. They're not hurting anything."

"They're little O.R. kids," she tried to explain.

"They have just as much right to play on the sidewalk as you have to leave—which, by the way, you're doing now."

"I didn't realize I was leaving."

"Oh, you are, honey, you are—or I'm calling the cops." In case she thought I was joking, I added, "Go on, get out of here."

No one was going to trip Emily on my watch.

I went over to Emily and Chelsey and started talking to them. "I don't want you to think all adults are like that," I said.

"Hi, I'm Emily."

"And I'm Chelsey."

"Well, hello there, sugars. I'm Miss Norma. I work here at the clinic. I'm one of the counselors, so you'll probably see me out here a lot. I like little kids, and I don't like anybody mistreating them."

"Then why are you letting the little ones die inside?" Emily asked.

I never answered her. I couldn't. This little girl was the only person in the world who could have gotten away with saying something like that to me. Instead of spewing my usual obscenities in her face, I turned and walked inside the clinic without saying another word.

I thought that was it between me and Emily. I was so certain that her mom had painted me out to be the wicked witch of the east, she would never want to talk to me again. But the next time I saw Emily, she came up and hugged me.

I was as pleased as I was confused. A hug was the last thing I expected from her, but later, I came to realize that's just Emily's way. She will tell you exactly what she thinks, but she won't stop loving you even if you disagree.

Thus began my friendship with Emily. We spent hours outside, playing and chatting. And always, I was greeted by a hug. Emily gives the best hugs. She has skinny little arms, and she reaches up on tiptoe to grab me around my neck. Her hugs were always strong enough to let me know her heart was in each one, but soft enough to resemble a caress.

I didn't know it at the time, but Emily was on her way to hugging me into the kingdom.

An Untimely Pregnancy

It was a difficult thing for Ronda to let the relationship between Emily and me build. For you to understand my story, you must also understand Ronda's story, for this is where another one of those ironies comes together. Emily, the girl who helped lead Jane Roe to the Lord, was almost aborted.

In December 1986 Ronda was twenty years old and living a carefree life. She was told that because of her many medical problems she could never bear children, at least not without the help of a specialist. Many of her friends had gotten pregnant several times and had opted for abortions.

Ronda used her condition as an excuse to enjoy what she thought would be consequence-free sex. She moved in with her boyfriend in Colorado, and the two of them planned to get engaged. On Christmas Day, the two announced their formal plans to marry.

Within days, Ronda noticed that her period was late, but she did not give it much thought until they were making plans to celebrate the new year. Their usual custom on New Year's Eve was to get wildly drunk; now Ronda thought that if there was a chance she could be pregnant, getting smashed might not be the best way to celebrate the coming year.

When Ronda told her fiancé that she didn't plan to drink anything that night, a terrible fight ensued, but Ronda remained insistent. The next day—January 1, 1987—Ronda took a pregnancy test.

It was positive.

Ronda's boyfriend was furious. Since she had told him she could not get pregnant, he never bothered with birth control. For months he had thought living with Ronda was great fun. Now he felt that he had been cheated and misled, and he put the entire blame on Ronda.

Ronda was upset too. She had no desire to raise a child. The thought of becoming a mother at her age seemed overwhelming. Her fiancé finally got over his anger long enough to see that Ronda was genuinely anxious and scared—maybe she really hadn't planned this, he realized—so he softened and called his parents for advice.

"Mom, Dad," he began, "Ronda's pregnant."

There was a long silence on the other end of the line. Finally, his mother said, "Listen. You need to take care of this problem right away. This is not the way to start out a marriage. The first year you need to travel, you need to have fun and get to know one another, and you can't do that with a baby."

The advice made sense to Ronda and she readily agreed to "take care of the problem right away," but later that night she could not rid her mind of a troubling memory. Back in high school, Ronda's best friend had moved out of town; at her new school, she was elected lieutenant of the drill team. Shortly thereafter, Ronda's friend found out she was pregnant. Her mother brought her back to Dallas to get an abortion—after all, she couldn't let something like an unborn baby get in the way of her daughter finally accomplishing a goal of becoming lieutenant of the drill team.

The friend's mother was determined to keep news of the abortion from her husband (the girl's stepfather), so she arranged to have her daughter stay with Ronda for two weeks, to make it look like a social visit. Of course, Ronda was eager to spend time again with her best friend. Though Ronda knew why her friend was coming back to Dallas, the thought of her getting an abortion did not bother Ronda at all.

After the abortion, the mother dropped Ronda's friend off. Ronda greeted her warmly, but she realized within minutes that her friend was a very different young woman from the one she had known just months before. For starters, she cried morning, noon, and night.

The friend would drench Ronda's pillow with her tears, then escape to the bathroom where she would cry some more. Ronda tried to comfort her, but her friend refused to be comforted. "I can't believe I killed my baby," she said. "I just can't believe it."

At the time, Ronda ached for her friend, but also for herself. She remembered the doctor's words, "You'll probably never be able to bear children," and she found herself promising, "Look, if you get pregnant again, give the baby to me. I'll raise it."

But now, a couple of years later, when she was the one who was pregnant, Ronda could not believe that abortion was foremost in her mind. She was not supposed to be able to bear children. In many ways, this child was a miracle—so how could she abort it? In her friend's words, she would be killing it.

Ronda knew it was a baby. She was not a Christian at the time, so theology played absolutely no role in her thinking about abortion. But, intuitively, she knew that a child was growing inside her. This was much more than a "missed period" (one of the abortion movement's favorite descriptions) floating around in her stomach. This was a child, her child.

She finally went back to her boyfriend and said, "I'm sorry, but I can't do it. I can't get an abortion."

At first, her boyfriend argued with her, but when he realized that Ronda was not about to budge, he gave in. "Fine," he said. "If that's the way you want it." He made it clear that he was not happy about her decision, but he agreed to move the wedding up two months. Ronda and her fiancé traveled to Kansas, got married, and began the first rocky months of a difficult union.

Midway through her pregnancy, Ronda began experiencing early contractions. The first thing the doctor asked her was, "Have you ever had an abortion?"

"No!" she answered emphatically.

"Then you must be under a lot of stress—marital, financial . . ."

"Both," Ronda confessed.

"Then that's it," the doctor told her. "A prior abortion is the most frequent cause of premature labor, but stress comes second."

Ronda marveled that none of her friends had been warned about this, nor had she. When she had considered an abortion, it never occurred to her that there would be long-term risks.

The doctor ordered her on immediate and complete bed rest. "If you don't stay in bed," he warned her, "there's a good chance you'll miscarry. The only reason you can get up is to use the bathroom. Other than that, you must stay in bed. Someone will have to feed you, bring you water, and something to read."

Ronda nodded. She and her husband had planned to go skiing that weekend, but she was sure he would understand.

He didn't.

"What do you mean, we can't go skiing?" he asked.

"Well, the doctor said I have to stay in bed. I'm not even supposed to fix my own meals, much less go skiing."

"Fine," he said. "You stay home, and I'll go skiing."

"But what about the bed rest? Who's going to fix my meals?"

"Listen, I've been looking forward to this skiing trip for a long time, and I'm going, so that's that."

Ronda started experiencing premature labor and phoned her mother.

"Look, honey," her mom told her, "a number of my friends went into premature labor, too, and it was for the best. Usually, premature labor is God's way of getting rid of a deformed baby. Don't take the medicine the doctor gave you to stop the contractions. Let nature take its course."

Ronda thought carefully about what her mother had said. It was one thing to abort a child for convenience, but maybe this situation was different. After all, her husband had no interest in the child and would be unsupportive, at best. And now she had reason to believe that perhaps the child was deformed. Perhaps the baby would be better off never being born.

Again, Emily's life hung in the balance. Ronda had lost the support of her husband and her mother. She was not at all sure that she could raise a child alone. For twenty-four long hours, she began to wonder if letting her baby die wouldn't be the best way to get out of a situation that was bad and could be headed for worse.

But something inside her would not let her do it. Ronda reached out, took the doctor's medication, and decided to remain on bed rest.

A Reluctant Mother

The eighth month of Ronda's pregnancy finally arrived, and so did the beginning of labor. Ronda was back in Dallas, and her husband had been traveling, so Ronda phoned him to make sure he would return in time for the delivery. He arrived in Dallas, and the wait began. That night, Ronda's contractions became more forceful and frequent. She called the doctor, who told her to get to the hospital.

"Looks like we'll have a baby in the morning," he said.

Ronda went in to wake up her husband. A contraction hit just as she walked in, so she paused, breathed through the contraction, then approached the bed and gently shook her husband's shoulder. "I just called the doctor," she said. "He said I should come in right away."

Ronda's husband looked up at her, nodded, sighed, then rolled back over. His angry look frightened Ronda. She felt particularly vulnerable, experiencing the pangs of labor and needing help from a man who resented her condition; so she let him sleep for another thirty minutes, hoping his conscience would stir him.

As the contractions grew more forceful, Ronda knew she had to get to the hospital, which was forty-five minutes away. She breathed through another contraction, approached her husband one last time, and pleaded, "Please, I really need to go to the hospital. Now."

Without saying a word, he got up and took her to the hospital. Ronda gave birth a few hours later, early in the morning. She expected to see a beautiful, pink, healthy-looking little girl. Her heart sank when she beheld a grotesquely skinny child, covered in the white mucous that surrounds all preemies, who had to be immediately whisked away for treatment. The sight was so stark, there was absolutely no bonding.

The entire pregnancy had been such a lonely, overwhelming ordeal that Ronda could scarcely believe it was over. She was completely unprepared for motherhood. Her goal had been, "I've just got to get this child born," but with that accomplished, she now showed no interest in her newborn.

The nurses kept bringing Emily in all day long, asking if Ronda wanted to hold her. "No, I can't see her right now," Ronda said.

She did not miss the nurses' disapproving looks, but she was too tired to care. Later, the nurses became more insistent. "The baby is very hungry," they pleaded. "Please, she needs to eat."

"Then give her a bottle," Ronda snapped. "I don't want her right now."

The tears came next. Wave upon wave upon wave poured out of Ronda. The blackness of depression enveloped her completely, and she fought just to stay sane. This lasted for two full days. Ronda's depression was so deep, the doctor refused to authorize her release.

Finally, in the middle of the night, Ronda woke up from a restless sleep and decided she wanted to hold Emily. She got out of bed, walked to the nursery, and knocked on the nurses' window.

"What do you need?" they asked.

"I want to see my baby."

Ronda knew it was against hospital policy for them to bring the baby out at that time, but they were so thankful Ronda was finally showing some interest in Emily, they practically tackled one another in an attempt to get Emily into Ronda's arms before she changed her mind.

That night, Emily slept in the arms of her mother and Ronda finally bonded with her child. The next morning, the attending nurse still approached Ronda gingerly. "Ready for some classes?" she asked tentatively.

"Yes," Ronda shot back, "I'm ready to do it all," and she heard the nurse breathe a huge sigh of relief.

A New Start

Unfortunately, this was not a marriage that ends with "and they lived happily ever after." Ronda's husband never did fully accept his responsibility as a father, and he left Ronda when Emily was just six weeks old.

"I thought I wanted to be married," he told Ronda. "I thought I wanted children, but I guess I was wrong. Now all I want is out."

He broke all contact and refused to pay any child support. Ronda was crushed, but when she went to her mom to get sympathy, she was told, "Look, Ronda, if you make your bed hard, you learn to lie in it." So that's what Ronda did.

In spite of her future sweet disposition, Emily, as a preemie, was not an easy child to care for. Her crying spells were frequent and exhausting, and Ronda sleepwalked her way through many a workday. She came home, fed Emily, gave her a bath, and then immediately dropped into bed as soon as Emily dozed off. On average, Emily slept about two hours, after which Ronda spent about forty-five minutes feeding and changing her, then laid her gently back into the crib for another precious hour or so of sleep.

This went on for over two years. Emily eventually slept through the night, Ronda aged about a decade in maturity, and a new man, named Ron, came into her life. On their second date, Ron took Ronda to church and led her to the Lord.

At first, Ronda was skeptical about Ron's interest. She had been so burned by her failed marriage, she was in no hurry to rush into another. Besides, Ron wasn't really her type. But as the days passed into weeks and the weeks turned into months, Ronda was won over by this man who treated Emily so warmly. He helped cut Emily's food at restaurants. At night, when he was over at Ronda's apartment, he would read Emily a story, then carry her to bed, where he prayed with her. In short, he was the father Emily never had, and when he asked Ronda to marry him, Ronda felt all the emotions a prospective bride should. "Yes!" she said, and their new life had begun.

Ronda's first husband eventually came around and began paying child support and taking more interest in his daughter. Even so, Emily was thrilled when Ron became her father. She told Ronda, "I'm so glad you met Daddy, because if you hadn't, we would both be going to hell right now." Even at three years old, Emily had figured out that Ronda's lifestyle was not right.

And now, at age seven, Emily was about to turn that insight on me!

CHAPTER 15

Out of the Mouths of Babes . . .

After Ronda became a Christian, she turned into an ardent pro-lifer. I suppose it was inevitable that, even though she didn't know me, I became her enemy. What I had done, signing the affidavit that made abortion legal, had hit too close to home. To Ronda, I was the cause of legalized abortion. I was the main reason Emily was almost never born and the reason Ronda's friend had changed so dramatically. Besides, if it weren't for me, Ronda would not have had to spend all her hours volunteering for Operation Rescue!

In short, I was public enemy number one, and Ronda was not at all pleased when little Emily began talking about her "new friend," Miss Norma. But just as Emily had backed me up against a wall, she backed her mother up against another wall. Emily loves to love others; that's who she is. And Ronda began to wonder, *Am I supposed to teach my daughter that some people aren't worthy to be loved? Is that really the lesson God wants me to pass on?*

So Ronda allowed my friendship with Emily and Chelsey to continue, even allowing her daughters to visit me at the clinic, with one condition.

"Miss Norma," she said, "you must never—ever—take Emily or Chelsey in the back (where the abortions were performed). Understand?"

"I don't like to go there myself," I said. "I'll have them stay in the reception area, where they can watch television."

"Okay. Then they can visit you."

I caught myself looking forward to the kids' first visit. The clinic could be a dreary place, and these children seemed to lighten everything up. Chelsey didn't stay for long, however. Within minutes she excused herself, then ran back to Ronda's office, complaining, "I don't like it over there. It's spooky."

Emily sat quietly in my office, coloring pictures, softly singing and—unknown to me—spying. We watched a little of *Jeopardy* on television, and I would call out the answers when the questions came up.

"Miss Norma!" Emily said, clearly astonished. "You're so smart!"

As the day wore on, I forgot Emily was even there as I went about my work. Women called to make appointments, and I got as mad as ever. One girl called in and asked how much it would cost to get an abortion.

"That depends, honey," I replied. "How far along are you?"

"Twenty-one weeks," she said.

"Twenty-one weeks?" I repeated. "That'll cost one thousand, two hundred dollars. But you'll have to come in early, on Thursday, to have laminaria put in, and then you can have the abortion on Friday."

"Why? My friend had an abortion at twenty-six weeks, and she didn't have to come in early."

"You need the laminaria to open your cervix so the procedure can be performed. It's safer that way."

"But I don't want to come in early. I just want to come in once."

This went on for some time until I grew tired of it and said, "Look, I'm not gonna argue with you. I'd just as soon see you in hell as see you in here."

She hung up the phone before I could hang up on her. As I dropped the phone from my ear, I saw Emily and wanted to shoot myself.

"You don't have to go to hell, Miss Norma," Emily said politely. "You can pray right now, and Jesus will forgive you."

I felt like I was half an inch tall. I never pretended to be someone other than who I was, and that was a sinner extraordinaire. What was I doing with an innocent child in my office?

A Guided Tour

That evening, Ronda came over to our clinic to pick up Emily. She knocked on the door (we kept it locked to keep out the "terrorists"), but nobody answered. A few minutes later, I walked around the corner with Emily.

Ronda shot me a look that blazed fire. At first, I didn't understand what I had done, then I realized she misunderstood. We had come out of the back door, so Ronda assumed I had taken Emily into the back room where the procedures were performed. "We were in my office," I explained quickly, "not the procedure room. She never saw it."

"That's true, Mommy," Emily said, and Ronda's ice-cold glare warmed, though just slightly. I was anxious not to lose Emily's or Ronda's friendship so I offered, without thinking, "Here, let me show you."

Ronda was shocked. I suppose I should have been too. I was inviting a member of Operation Rescue to tour our offices. It was ridiculous, on the face of it.

Ronda's incredulous look gave way to a smile. Later, she told me that she was eager to see our offices because they often placed their hands against the walls and prayed. Now she would finally get to see exactly what rooms they were praying for.

When Ronda walked into my office, she saw Emily and Chelsey's artwork: the crosses, the "I Love You, Miss Norma" posters, the "Jesus Loves You, Miss Norma" posters, and it took her breath away.

"I had no idea," she said. Her voice was soft, and sounded faraway, as if she was deep in thought. Something was happening inside her, but I didn't know what.

Ten minutes later, Ronda walked out of my office with Emily and Chelsey holding each of her hands. Before they were even around the corner, Emily called out, "Mama, I know a girl that's twenty-one weeks, and she's coming to get an abortion!"

I had been making appointments all afternoon, and Emily, bless her heart, was busy memorizing all the pertinent information. She was willing to show kindness to me, but there was never any doubt about whose side she was on!

"Shhhh," Ronda warned her. "We'll talk about it later. Not here."

I heard none of this.

Ronda and the girls piled into the van and Ronda paused before starting it up. "Now what did you hear?"

"What does twenty-one weeks mean?" Emily asked. "That's too young to be pregnant, isn't it?"

"That's how old the baby is," Ronda explained. "You're sure you heard twenty-one weeks?"

"It costs over a thousand dollars!" Emily explained. "And she's coming in on Thursday!"

Ronda filed this information away and thought, *Maybe Emily's going next door isn't such a bad idea after all.* Soon Emily became a staple in our clinic, at least on non-procedure days. She didn't want to be there when abortions were taking place, and to be honest, that was the only time I didn't want her to be around, either.

Putting on the Armor

On Ronda's drive to work, she and her daughters went through a daily ritual. First, Emily would pray: "Dear God, please don't let any babies be killed, and make it so that abortion will end. Help Miss Norma to come to Jesus and to quit smoking." She went on for several minutes, mentioning the abortion clinic workers by name. Next, Chelsey would lead in "putting on spiritual armor." Ronda was fully aware of the spiritual warfare into which she was leading her children, so every morning she wanted to make sure they donned their spiritual armor before arriving at the clinic.

Ronda grew increasingly concerned. Emily was at an impressionable age, and Ronda was afraid that her little girl would be disillusioned about prayer before she reached age ten. Ronda had heard my outbursts of anger and the filth that spewed out of my mouth. She thought I was the least likely convert in all of Dallas, if not the world.

"Emily," Ronda explained after one of Emily's prayers, "God always answers our prayers, but Miss Norma has a choice to make. She probably won't choose to follow Jesus. That's Miss Norma's fault, not God's. I don't want you to think God isn't listening to your prayers simply because Miss Norma doesn't become a Christian."

Emily smiled. "She's gonna come to know Jesus, Mama."

Apparently, Emily saw something that neither her mother nor I could see, but I was delighted to be around her. On one sunny day, I was walking out the door on a copy-making errand when I saw Emily playing by herself. "How would you like to ride in Bertha, and I'll buy you a coke?" I asked. (Bertha is the name of my truck.)

Emily squealed her delight. "I have to ask my mom."

"Go ahead. I'll wait."

As soon as Emily left my sight I thought, *Why in the world did I do that? I'm gonna get that poor girl all excited, and there's no way her mom will let her go with me.* It was one thing to be around Emily with her mother right next door. It was another thing altogether to ask her to take a truck ride with me. I wondered if I should leave right then to avoid the inevitable letdown. But I stayed, and Emily came out running.

"I can go! I can go!"

"Yippee!" I said, giving a big smile. But I was so surprised, I walked into the Rescue offices to double-check with Ronda.

"Did you understand what Emily wanted?"

"Yes."

"You understand we're leaving the property?"

"Yes. Just make sure she wears a seat belt."

Ronda and I had our differences, but I never looked at her in the same way after she trusted me with her firstborn. There's no way I was going to let down a woman who showed me that kind of trust.

I belted Emily into the truck and drove extra carefully. We finished the errands and chatted happily. Having Rescue move next door had created so much stress that it was wonderful to have fun again. I had done plenty of adult "entertainment"—getting drunk, staying out late in bars—but taking a seven-year-old girl out to get a soda was the most fun I had had in years.

Unknown to me at the time, Ronda was back in the Rescue offices, looking like she had lost a couple of pints of blood.

"What is it?" a volunteer asked.

"I let Emily take a drive with Miss Norma."

Several volunteers gathered around and began praying for Ronda. Ronda responded by repeating several times out loud, "She doesn't belong to me, she belongs to the Lord. She doesn't belong to me, she belongs to the Lord."

A Mother's Heart

"We're going to my house first," I explained to Emily. "I have a kitty there."

"Oooooh," Emily said. I smiled.

When we walked into my living room, I sat Emily down on the couch and asked her not to move. I had stopped using drugs, but I didn't want her to accidentally come across anything that might have been left lying around.

"Okay, Miss Norma," she said in her singsong voice.

I came back out a few minutes later, and my heart melted when I saw Emily sitting quietly on the couch, her legs crossed at the ankles. I wanted to cry. A maternal side of me that had long laid dormant was being resurrected.

You see, though I had been pregnant three times, I was never allowed to be much of a mom. In fact, my first pregnancy almost ended before I gave birth. My husband beat me severely when he found out I was pregnant, insinuating that the child was not his. And then, shortly after I gave birth, I had my child literally stolen by my mother when I confessed to her that I was a lesbian. I was drunk one evening, she asked me to sign some papers (which I didn't read), and I was shocked to find out later that I had been tricked into placing Melissa entirely under her care.

My second pregnancy ended in a closed adoption. When I woke up from the delivery, the child was already gone. The third child, my *Roe* baby, was also adopted, but that was a particularly heartbreaking one. The nurse on duty made a mistake and brought the baby into my room. I broke down and cried, the nurse realized her mistake and whisked the child away, but not before I saw a beautiful baby girl. That sight haunted me for years afterward.

In short, though I've always had a mother's instinct and have often been accused of being a "mother hen," my attempts at mothering always ended in disaster. But with Emily, I was able to act as a surrogate mom, and it elicited strange new emotions. Children—my children, anyway—had always come at inconvenient times. I had viewed their conceptions with alarm and their births with dread.

But when I saw Emily, I saw a child, not a problem. I saw a miracle, not an inconvenience. I saw joy and laughter, and I ached for what I had done.

Emily's visits became frequent. In fact, I went to the clinic more often just to see Emily—I couldn't go a day without one of her hugs.

The first picture Emily made for me was of a boat sailing underneath a very sunny sky (the sun always shines for Emily). I now keep the boat picture in my bedroom, and it's more precious to me than many of the originals I have. It's the first thing I see every morning when I wake up. That bright sun reminds me of Emily's bright smile. Inside the rolling waves, I see Emily's wrinkled nose.

Who would have thought that Jane Roe would ever be so sentimental about a child's drawing? Yet it was this child's love and interest that began to melt my heart. Soon this love would constitute an all-out assault.

CHAPTER 16

Assaulted by Love

On the second Saturday of every month, the Christians would come out and stand in front of the abortion clinic and pray. I previously avoided the clinic on these days, but I knew I had to show up once O.R. moved in, as extra administrative oversight would be crucial.

When I arrived at the clinic one Saturday, I was reminded of just how difficult our task had become. The O.R. protesters were using our own parking lot to park their cars; technically, it was their lot too. Women coming in for their abortions had to pass bumper stickers all along the way:

"Abortion Stops a Beating Heart."

"Aren't You Glad Mary and Joseph Were Pro-Life?"

"Abortion: American Holocaust."

"Abortion: One Dead, One Wounded."

"It's a Child, Not a Choice."

As I surveyed the situation and got a feel for what was going on, I became more angry at Arnie, the abortionist, than at anyone else. The women working at the clinic were continually forced to deal with O.R. themselves while the doctor stayed huddled safely inside, away from the circus that had descended on north Dallas. Well, if he would not take action, I guessed it would have to be me.

I walked outside and shouted, "I thought y'all wanted to keep the law!"

Somebody shouted back, "God's law, not man's law."

I shrugged my shoulders. "What's the difference?"

I stood off to one side and watched the hullabaloo until I couldn't take it anymore. My anger snapped. I remembered how, three years earlier, I had picketed a Rescue event and the police had told me that I couldn't park my car on the same property I was picketing, so now I walked up to Anne Hollacher, an O.R. volunteer holding a picket sign, and yelled, "You can't park on the same place you're picketing. Move the car!"

"No, I am not moving my car," she responded. "This is our parking lot too."

I called her every name you've ever heard, then made up some for good measure. That was usually enough to make the toughest protesters wilt, but Anne maintained her composure. When she refused to step back, I spit in her face.

Anne smiled.

Now I was furious. I could barely contain myself. "How dare you look at me like that," I screamed. "How dare you smile at me!"

Anne politely wiped the spit off her face with her sleeve. "Jesus loves you, and so do I," she said. "And I forgive you."

That was it. I declared war on this poor woman, and soon I was all over her. I started getting physical, shoving her around, cussing her out, and knocking her sign to the ground. Anne picked up the sign as if nothing but a gust of wind had pulled it from her hand. I could not believe it.

Then, in an instant, I felt like someone had taken a sledgehammer to my chest. I crossed my hands over my chest and started leaning back. Chest pains are always terrifying, especially sudden ones.

At that moment, Ronda and the two girls drove up. My first thought was, *I'm so glad the girls didn't see what I just did.* I would have died if Emily had heard my filthy language or watched me hit another person.

I had to get out of there, fast, so I slipped away to the back of the clinic and lit up a cigarette.

The chest pains subsided somewhat, but I was still having a difficult time settling down and breathing when I heard Ronda's two little girls running around the corner. They had watched me walk back and were eager to greet me: "Good morning, Miss Norma. Are you having a good morning?"

Ronda didn't normally bring her children to the offices on Saturdays; it was just too crazy, and she didn't want them there to see it. But Emily was determined to give me my daily hug, and she couldn't do that if her mother left her behind.

"Please?" she had asked Ronda. "Can't I go?"

"No, Emily, you're not going. I have my reasons, and I don't want you there."

But when Ronda got up early in the morning to slip out the door, she discovered that Emily had crawled out of bed in the middle of the night, gotten dressed—including her shoes—and had lain down by the front door so her mother could not go without her. For some reason, Emily felt she *had* to be there that day.

Ronda finally relented. For my sake, I'm glad she did.

"I'm Not Coming Back!"

I was huffing and puffing, holding my chest, as the girls called out their greetings. Ronda followed behind them. She took one look at me, and her eyes grew wide. *Do I look that bad?* I wondered.

"Miss Norma," Ronda said, "I can tell you're not having a good day."

I snapped at her. "Oh, how did you figure that one out, Ronda?" My voice was full of sarcasm. I had not yet learned how to turn my anger off, and it pretty much came out indiscriminately once I got going.

Emily and Chelsey never flinched. They came up on the porch and hugged me and greeted me in their high, tiny voices.

It broke my heart. I thought I would explode. All week long Ronda and the girls and I were best friends, but whenever abortions were performed, we became bitter enemies. I couldn't take it anymore.

I went back into the clinic and shouted, "I can't deal with this crap anymore. I'm not coming back ever again. Don't even ask me to come back."

Of course I stayed. I had to do something with my anger, though, so I sought out Arnie and threw him up against a wall, shaking my finger in his face.

"This has to stop," I told him. "You're not a man, you're just a little cardboard cutout. You should do something. It's a circus out there, but you leave it all to the women. You're always hiding behind a woman's skirts."

Arnie was stunned. He knew I had a temper to match an elephant, but I had given him a year and a half of dedicated service, and he had never seen anything like this. What he did not understand was that, for once, my upheaval was spiritual. I didn't realize it back then, but the hounds of heaven were biting at my heels. I didn't like it one bit.

I stayed in my office, fuming that we had been left to cope with Operation Rescue alone. Nobody from NOW, the Choice Foundation, or the gay and lesbian community had come to help us. Dallas has a local chapter of just about every liberal-leaning organization known to mankind, but we were left to fend for ourselves.

Finally, one of the people from the Choice Foundation did come by to see how things were going. She went into the doctor's office, where a woman was waiting to be counseled, and stood on Arnie's desk. She then pushed up the ceiling tile so she could peek into O.R.'s office and "get a feel for what was going on."

Of course, all she saw was crawl space.

I walked into Arnie's office, saw the patient sitting there with a horrified look on her face, Arnie standing meekly off to the side, and the woman from the Choice Foundation standing on top of his desk. She was not a small woman, by any means, and it was not a pretty sight.

Though it sounds comical now, it didn't seem so funny at the time, and I thought, *The entire world has gone crazy on me.* I had enough on my hands without receiving help like this!

"Come down from there," I said. "I'm going to go mad. It's going to kill me to put up with this mess."

I escorted the woman out the door and thought, *Maybe we're better off without any help.*

As soon as the woman had left, I locked the front door and realized to my horror that I was losing it. Two beautiful children were right outside, both of whom loved me dearly; we played together Monday through Wednesday, exchanged kisses and hugs, gave each other gifts, but then were on "opposite sides" Thursday through Saturday. I hated it.

This is not worth six bucks an hour, I said to myself. Though Arnie made a very good living, the money was not passed down, believe me. The women at the clinic worked more out of a sense of duty than financial gain.

I got into my truck and drove home, downed a few beers, and then started weeping uncontrollably. *I can't continue to do this*, I kept moaning. *I've got to stop.* I began sweating profusely and trembling.

Then, virtually out of nowhere, I caught myself whispering, "God, help me, please. Tell me what to do, and I'll do it. I can't continue to fight this battle."

I thought it extremely bizarre that I should even mention God's name. I usually referred to the goddess. But something strange was happening inside me.

I closed my eyes to shut everything out, but all I could see was Emily's face, with her crinkled nose, and all I could hear was her singsong voice, "I love you, Miss Norma." It was killing me. Ronda and I had become such good friends, but she was supposed to be the enemy.

In truth, though at the time I didn't know it, I was being won by love. I could handle the hatred. When people yelled at me and called me a murderer and a wicked witch and things that shouldn't be printed—that didn't affect me. I could handle that. But the love in Ronda's face, and the love pouring out of Emily's voice—well, that love just about ripped me apart.

When Connie came home later in the day I told her, "Look, I can't go back. I'll come in on Monday and Tuesday, but not during procedure days." Connie nodded, and I kept drinking, but I couldn't get Emily's and Chelsey's faces out of my mind.

The weekend was an amalgam of drinking, passing out, crying myself back to sleep, then waking up to the sound of Emily's "I love you, Miss Norma," followed by a drinking binge to make the pain stop. I purposefully avoided drugs, for fear that I would almost certainly overdose, but the drinking was bad, even for me. I'd sort of wake up, find myself in the middle of the dining room, and think, *Okay, I remember coming in here,* then pass out again and wake up somewhere else.

It was horrible, but I was fighting against a powerful new foe, and I felt helpless. I didn't know how to cope, how to overcome the strange draw this child's love represented. And how could a child love *me,* anyway? What kind of irony was this? I was Jane Roe, the national enemy of children, the one responsible for the deaths of over thirty-five million of them before they were born.

Didn't Emily know that? Didn't she realize who I was? Of course she did. So why did she still love me? Why did she still paint me pictures and sing me songs and look so happy to see me?

I couldn't figure it out. The truth is, I was defeated, and I knew it. But I was not about to let go. Not yet, anyway.

CHAPTER 17

Rescue Raided

On April 19, 1995, twenty minutes before Timothy McVeigh set off a bomb in Oklahoma City, a constable accompanied by several women marched into the Rescue offices and told Ronda, "We need a check for 1.2 million dollars."

Ronda laughed.

"We're serious. You give us a check, or we'll confiscate your furniture. Immediately."

Ronda's face fell. She knew what this was about. Three years prior, Operation Rescue organized a prayer vigil on a public sidewalk across the street from a Planned Parenthood abortion clinic. The prayer vigil was held during the Republican National Convention in Houston, Texas, where a huge fight was brewing over the Republican platform.

Though the Rescue people remained on the sidewalk across the street, engaged only in prayer, and never once entered the private property of Planned Parenthood, they were sued by Planned Parenthood under the new FACE Act.

At first, Rescue leaders did not take the lawsuit too seriously. Surely, in America, you could not be sued for praying across the street from an abortion clinic while standing on a public sidewalk.

True to form, however, our nation's federal courts sided with Planned Parenthood and awarded them $1.2 million. When the judgment was first announced, I danced a little celebratory jig, just like all the abortion clinic workers, but that was before I knew the Rescue people firsthand.

Ronda looked at the abortion workers who were standing next to the constable—two Houston women from Planned Parenthood, their lawyer, and a woman who worked for the local Choice Foundation. If Ronda had so much as driven by their offices, she could be arrested; yet here they were, standing in O.R.'s headquarters, demanding a check for over a million dollars!

"I want those people out of here," she said, pointing to the abortion workers.

"They have every right to be here," the constable explained. "Everything you have belongs to them now."

Ronda lost it. She's a strong woman, but she had worked night and day to get the O.R. office up and running. She had sacrificed many afternoons and many evenings to help Flip build an efficient operation on a shoestring budget—and now her enemies, the abortionists, were going to take it all away.

It was too much. She started crying hysterically, pleading with the constable, "I want those people out of here. Please, make them leave."

The constable would not budge. "No. They have every right to be here, and they're going to stay."

Soon, however, Ronda's display of heartfelt emotion softened the constable's heart and he instructed the abortion workers to wait outside.

"Can I at least keep the petty cash?" she asked when she was finally calm enough to speak.

"How much do you have in there?"

"Less than ten dollars."

"Go ahead."

"What about our files?"

"Two trucks are now on their way. When those two trucks get here, whatever is in the desks goes out with them. Whatever you can get out of the file cabinets and desks before they arrive, you can keep."

Another O.R. volunteer, Dennis Alexander, walked into the offices and Ronda quickly explained their crisis. The two began dialing numbers like crazy. "You've got to come down to our offices now," they told supporter after supporter. "As soon as the trucks get here, Planned Parenthood is going to take everything we have."

You have never seen a paper rush like the one that went on that morning. Word spread quickly. Men and women left their jobs, mothers brought their children, and people poured into the Rescue offices. Files were literally dumped on the floor. There was no time to neatly organize them or transfer them to boxes. Besides, any box could be claimed by the Planned Parenthood people as their "property."

Some computer-literate men began furiously copying the mailing list and erasing the data so that it could not be retrieved. The minutes ticked by. I heard all the commotion but, like most of the country, was absorbed by the news surrounding Oklahoma City; so I stayed in my office, my eyes glued to the television set.

Finally, we heard the front bell go off. One of the women from Planned Parenthood asked for me, and when I went out to meet her, she said, "How much longer are you going to be on the property?"

"I don't think that's any of your business," I said.

"We're taking over O.R.'s possessions and have scheduled a news conference later in the day. I'm afraid that if you're on the property, you will become the focus of the conference, and we don't want that."

"You're crazy if you think you'll find anything of value over there."

Actually, I was just about to leave, but since she had asked me to go, I decided to stick around. Curious to see what was going on, I went next door. As soon as I walked into Rescue's offices, I thought I was witnessing the aftermath of a tornado.

Paper was everywhere. People were moving at a furious pace, but there seemed to be little purpose to their frantic activity. They were like a bunch of ants climbing over a piece of melon. Papers were dumped; a few men were huddled intently around a computer; and the whole atmosphere was one of barely contained panic.

"What's going on, guys?" I called out.

"Planned Parenthood came to collect," Ronda explained, pushing her hair back behind her left ear. I saw the sweat on her forehead. She looked hot, exhausted, stressed out, and tired.

I felt ashamed. Suddenly, the $1.2-million judgment seemed ridiculous to me. Over one million dollars to compensate Planned Parenthood for the "crime" of praying on a sidewalk across the street from one of their clinics? When I had thought of O.R. as a group of fire-breathing terrorists, the inherent injustice of the verdict never bothered me, but now . . .

"I am so, so sorry," I said. And I meant it. I've been ripped off plenty of times, and theft leaves you with a terrible sense of invasion. From the looks of the O.R. office, this was without a doubt the ultimate rip-off, the worst I'd ever seen.

"I'm so sorry," I repeated, but Ronda didn't really have time to listen to me. She simply had to stay busy.

I went back to the clinic, and soon noticed the Planned Parenthood worker walking back toward our front door. She had the need of a bathroom written all over her face, so I quickly locked the front door and stood right behind it.

She jerked on the front door and frowned when she found out it was locked, then looked furious when she saw me smiling on the other side.

"Excuse me," she shouted, "I need to use the bathroom."

"Sorry," I said, "I'm afraid to open the door. The terrorists might come in. You'll have to walk down the street to the filling station."

The expression on her face would have curdled milk. She turned and stomped away. *Have a nice day,* I thought.

Abuse by any Other Name . . .

When the trucks arrived, the packers took everything. They might have missed a paper clip or two, perhaps a rubber band, but anything that had ten cents' worth of value was packed up and hauled away. I could see where the phone system had been taken out of the wall, wires left hanging. There was nothing but piles and piles of paper and files. I noticed they had not bothered to take the pro-life bumper stickers or the Focus on the Family counseling brochures.

To keep operating, Rick Blinn had gone out and purchased three phones. They turned two cardboard boxes over, and then removed a door from its hinges, laying it flat to create a makeshift desk to hold the phones.

"Ronda," I said, trying to comfort her, but stopped. For the first time since I had known her, the light in her eyes had dimmed. "I've got a fax machine. You can use it until you figure out a way to get a new one."

Ronda looked at me with one of the most bizarre expressions I've ever seen, and for good reason. By all accounts, I should have been clicking my heels together and joining in the celebration. Planned Parenthood had won. Operation Rescue had lost. You could even say that there was no Operation Rescue anymore, not really—just some massive, disorganized piles of paper and three brand-new phones.

The media had been tipped off and were swarming over the property now. Boom trucks pierced the skyline, and photographers were clicking cameras everywhere you turned. It was clear that the reporters were enjoying this—they had covered Operation Rescue's move-in day, and now, just a few weeks later, they were reporting O.R.'s supposed dismantling.

I was surprised by how upset I became. It was one thing for *me* to verbally abuse, harass, and otherwise make their lives mis-

Enjoying the view from the pier in Santa Monica, California, in May of 1989, shortly after I stopped using drugs.

On the NBC set with Holly Hunter, the actress who portrayed me in the made-for-TV movie, *Roe v. Wade*.

My former attorney and friend, Gloria Allred, as we enjoy coffee at an outdoor cafe in November of 1989

The Operation Rescue Group celebrates the closing of the A to Z Women's Clinic in Dallas, Texas, early in the spring of 1995.

An Operation Rescue worker, with seven-year-old Emily Mackey at his side, tries to speak to the girls in the Choice for Women waiting room to offer them hope.

Once Operation Rescue relocated next to the Choice for Women clinic, the police were always on the alert for possible confrontations.

Flip Benham, director of Operation Rescue National, baptizes me in the pool of a private home in North Garland, Texas, on August 8, 1995.

The sidewalk counselors and members of Hillcrest Church, my new church family, participate in the baptism service.

Emily drives her sister, Chelsey, around in her new Barbie jeep, which was given to her by some of the employees at the Choice for Women clinic for her eighth birthday in September of 1995.

Chelsey, myself, Meredith Champion, and Ronda Mackey in front of the North Dallas Women's Clinic where Ronda found baby Malachi in February of 1996.

Chelsey and I participate in our first "block and walk" during a Jericho Walk, a walk around an abortion clinic in Chicago, Easter 1996. Both of us were scared to death, especially when a policeman came up to us and said, "Do you two girls want to go to jail?" Ronda, Chelsey's mom, and Bob Behn, an Operation Rescue leader from New York, stood with us.

Presidential candidate Alan Keyes and I speak at a rally outside of Dallas City Hall on the 23rd anniversary of *Roe v. Wade*.

A Memorial Service for the Unborn at Georgetown University on January 21, 1996. Reverend Rob Schenck, general secretary to the National Clergy Council, myself, Flip Benham, Randall Terry, founder of Operation Rescue, and Reverend Johnny Hunter, national director of Learn (Life Education and Resource Network).

Flip Benham and I went to Washington, D.C., in April of 1996 to present copies of the video "Reversing Roe" to the Supreme Court justices.

A rally in front of Dallas City Hall on January 22, 1997, the 24th anniversary of *Roe v. Wade*. I am reading the "Empty Playgrounds" poem.

Sandra Cano, Mary Doe in *Doe v. Bolton* (a case that authorized abortions through all nine months of pregnancy), and I dedicate plaques at the National Memorial for the Unborn in Chattanooga, Tennessee, in 1997.

A hug from Emily, the precious little girl whose love changed one woman's life.

erable, but nobody else was going to do it. As far as I was concerned, these were my people to abuse, and it made me angry that someone else would wage such a petty war against them.

At least, that's what I told myself. Deep down, I had to admit that I really liked them, and I was genuinely moved by their hardship. They were my friends, and it hurt me to see them hurting.

But O.R. kept going. Much to my surprise, they didn't need my fax machine. When people heard what had happened, they became so indignant that donations of office equipment started pouring in from all over the country. The end result was that Planned Parenthood got a bunch of used, outdated, and largely dysfunctional office equipment and Operation Rescue got entirely new equipment and furniture.

The Landlord Fights Back

The next war waged against O.R. came from the landlord. He was furious that his office building had become the center ring in the ongoing circus battle between Operation Rescue and our abortion clinic. Though he had started it all by promising O.R. that A Choice for Women would eventually be forced to relocate, his attorneys had convinced him that, short of becoming extremely vulnerable to a lawsuit, there was nothing he could do to follow through on his promise to make us leave.

The only way to stop the circus, then, was to attack O.R. They were clearly the vulnerable ones now. Besides, after O.R. had been slapped with a $1.2 million judgment, the landlord did not expect they would be able to pay any kind of rent.

Still, there was that pesky contract . . .

So the landlord got creative. Now that the weather was getting hot, he cut off the air-conditioning to O.R.'s offices. Keep in mind, this was the beginning of the summer. In Dallas. And the office had one window that did not open and only the open front door for air circulation.

Our abortion clinic, right next door, was mysteriously spared from all these air-conditioning malfunctions. The O.R. offices became a sweatshop, and the thought of Emily and Chelsey, with their bangs sweat-plastered to their foreheads, trying to drink enough ice water to keep from overheating, was enough to motivate me to make a special trip into the O.R. offices to see how they were doing.

When I walked through the door, I couldn't believe how hot it was inside. It felt like 110 degrees. How on earth could these Christians get any work done?

"Ronda," I said, "why don't you let me take the girls next door where it's cool?"

Ronda was grateful for my offer, and I spent even more time fretting over the growing mixed emotions within me. Everyone, it seemed, was against Operation Rescue: Planned Parenthood, the media, and now the landlord. So why wasn't I happy? Why was I getting angrier by the second? And why was I watching her kids at my abortion clinic—taking time out from making appointments—so Ronda could keep working for Operation Rescue?

"What's with These People?"

When the lack of air-conditioning didn't force O.R. out, the landlord resorted to intimidation. He hired two burly men to harass the O.R. workers who stood outside to counsel prospective abortion patients.

"Who are those ugly lugs?" I asked Connie one day. They looked mean from a mile away.

"The landlord hired them," Connie said, smiling. "They're supposed to make life difficult for the Christians."

The two men played loud rap music so our clients could not hear the Christians' pleas, but they quickly cut the music when no clients were in sight and then whispered their juiciest obscenities at the most pious-looking women they could find. Sometimes they would even lean over and say, "You know, some evening, I'm gonna get you alone and I'm going to . . ."

The things they uttered were vile and disgusting. Even Connie couldn't handle it. "You should hear those guys out there," she told me. "They're nasty."

Occasionally I would hear them outside my office. Beavis and Butthead and Howard Stern sounded like three apostles by comparison. I marveled at how these determined young women did their best to ignore the threats, crude comments, and obscene sneers.

What is it with these Operation Rescue people? I kept asking myself. *They get thrown out, trampled on, robbed, shaken down, you name it, but nothing will stop them. Where does that strength come from?*

Suddenly, I wasn't sure which side I was on. Our clinic began receiving checks in the mail to help us in our "fight" with Operation Rescue. Without telling Arnie, I started sending the checks back. Almost without realizing it, I had begun to take O.R.'s side. If Ronda had to leave the building and walk to her car, Connie and I would escort her, talking loudly so she didn't have to listen to threats from the landlord's lackeys.

I still did my best to keep up appearances. I had to make them think I was tough, Jane Roe tough. I had my goddess, my pyramids, and my crystals to protect me. But for some reason, my spiritual armory was failing me. I would have to look elsewhere.

I had abused drugs for most of my life, and though lately I had begun to gain some mastery over them, I felt my willpower weakening.

Today, it only makes sense to me that my urge for drugs could at times be overpowering. Some clinics were such a macabre mess that you wanted to do drugs just to escape. Most people do not realize how unregulated abortion clinics are. The legal-abortion movement has hidden behind the slogan, "Keep abortion safe and legal," but the truth is, the *only* thing we fought for was legal abortion, not safe abortion. In fact, we fought tooth and nail against any attempt to impose even basic medical regulations, arguing that the very nature of choice was being attacked when the pro-lifers suggested the most modest of requirements.

Carol Everett, a former abortion clinic owner turned pro-lifer, tried to get a law passed in Texas that would require abortion clinics to meet the same regulations as veterinary clinics. The law finally passed in Texas in 1997 but only after several failures. Abortion has become the sacred cow of politics, and any attempt to regulate it seems doomed. You can't smoke while a German shepherd is being operated on, but you can have cigars aplenty while babies are being pulled out of their mothers' bodies, although that changed with the new law, at least in Texas.

To cope with what everyone intuitively knew were inhumane conditions, cocaine became a favorite pastime. At A to Z (where I worked before I took a position with Arnie), drugs became a major tool to keep the peace. Drugs got us through the day, and when memories kept us awake, drugs helped us get to sleep. When we couldn't bear the thought of going back for another day's worth of work, drugs got us out of bed.

We even used drugs with patients. Many times a young woman might say, "I'm not so sure I want to do this."

If the patient was holding things up, we knew just what to do. "Here, honey," we'd say, offering some cocaine. "Have a little hit of this. You'll be fine."

Our offer was not always accepted, but when it was, it worked wonders.

Because of the drugs, we knew we ran a risk every time we called the cops on pro-life protesters. Sometimes we put up with their harassment just because we thought it would be too much of an effort to clean up our own place. Whenever we called the police, we had to gather the straws and any containers used for drugs, and make sure they were hidden.

By sheer force of will, I had eventually broken my dependence on drugs by the time I came to work for Arnie. Of course,

I was still pretty much an alcoholic, but I had grown tired of putting about $30,000 worth of cocaine up my nose, and I did not want to go back to that.

But now, with so much stress, I felt the old familiar cravings, and I started making trips to the O.R. offices for no other reason than to ask for prayer. At first, they were suspicious of my requests, but after two or three times, they saw my sincerity.

"It's just that things go better when you pray," I explained to Flip.

He smiled and said, "Okay, Miss Norma, let me pray," then launched into his part. For some reason, this always comforted me.

I still did not believe in their God, but I did not want to resort to drugs, so I became willing to believe in their prayers. *Hey,* I thought to myself, *whatever works.* At the time, however, I had no idea how *well* their prayers were working. Had I known, I might never have asked them to continue.

CHAPTER 18

"Roe and Rescue Can't Be Friends . . . Can They?"

Miss Norma," *Flip* asked me one morning, "have you read your Bible today?"

"I don't have one," I confessed.

Flip stopped and looked at me. "Well, how about if I share a verse with you?"

"Whatever," I replied.

Flip sat down and looked me straight in the eyes. He has a way of doing it that completely catches you off guard. His stare goes right through you. It certainly helps him gather your attention, as his intensity becomes contagious.

"Miss Norma, did you know that God is pro-choice?"

"Say what?" I asked. "Excuse me, Flip. I haven't been drinking this morning, but I thought you just said that God is pro-choice."

"That's right, Miss Norma. He is."

What in the world is he talking about? I thought.

Flip opened his big Bible to Deuteronomy 30:19 and read: "I call heaven and earth as witnesses today against you, that I have set before you life and death, blessing and cursing; therefore choose life, that both you and your descendants may live."

"God wants us to choose," Flip explained. "He gives everyone a choice. God is the one who is truly pro-choice, and the choice he wants all of us to make is life."

The last thing I expected Mr. Flip Venom to tell me was that God, of all people, is pro-choice. Sure, he added the caveat that the choice had to be life; but still, I was getting confused.

Flip was like a fisherman. He would drop little worms of truth in front of me, just waiting for me to bite. I was not about to take the bait, but these conversations began building a sincere friendship—bizarre, but sincere.

A reporter from the *Fort Worth Star-Telegram* was the first one to pick up on our growing friendship, and that paper ran an article with a photograph showing us smiling at each other in front of the abortion clinic. The Associated Press picked up the article, including a photograph of Flip with his arm around my shoulder, and from there, the news went out all over the country.

"Norma McCorvey and Flip Benham, friendly neighbors?" asked the AP article, entitled "Friends in Enemy Country." "One might as well envision Grant and Lee sitting down to play bridge between battles."

When O.R. had first moved in, the media was there to cover a fight. Now my growing friendship with Flip had entered the "man bites dog" category of news—a completely unexpected twist on the normal pattern of events.

"What could you and Flip possibly have in common?" one reporter asked me. I thought for a moment and said, "Well, we both know where all the abortion clinics are!" The reporter and I had a good laugh over that one.

Once again, the media descended on us by the truckload. One young man looked incredulous as Flip and I kidded each other during the interview. "Roe and Rescue, friends?" he asked. "I just don't get it."

During this new season of heightened interest, a reporter actually helped set off my reevaluation of abortion. "Miss McCorvey, you've never had an abortion?" he asked me.

"No sir, I haven't."

"How funny that you work at an abortion clinic."

"I'm Jane Roe, I have every right to work anywhere I want to."

"But you've never had an abortion."

For some reason, the reporter's words just wouldn't leave my mind. "But you've never had an abortion. . . . But you've never had an abortion. . . ."

"Well so what!" I argued with him even after he had left. To a different reporter, I had once said I never had the *privilege* of aborting a baby, but something in this latest reporter's question led me to believe that *privilege* was not the best word.

Later that evening, after everybody had gone home, I thought to myself, *I'll show him.* I walked back to the procedure room and climbed onto the abortion table. I put my feet up into the stirrups and lay there for some time. Because I had assisted at so many abortions, I could visualize the entire procedure. I could see everybody standing around the room, going through the motions, and then I did something that caught me by surprise.

I started crying.

This is silly, I thought. I helped girls get over their crying all day long. What was I crying about? I was just sitting on a table, that's all.

I quickly replaced the crinkled paper with fresh paper, then went immediately to the phone to call my old dealer. I wanted drugs.

He wasn't home. I kept calling back until I reached him. "No, Norma," he said. "You asked me not to sell you any more, and I'm not going to."

"But you don't understand," I wanted to say, then realized how stupid that would sound. What could he not understand?

That I had climbed up on an operating table and suddenly had to have drugs?

In the back of my mind, I realized I had not climbed up on just *any* operating table. This was a table where abortions were performed. Something was going on inside me, but I didn't want to think about that. That's why I wanted the drugs, so I didn't have to feel, didn't have to think.

But I was soon to find out that as long as I remained a friend of Flip's, he was going to make me think—including what I thought about God.

CHAPTER 19

Spiritual Stuff

June 1995—the month before my conversion—must have been an incredibly busy time in heaven. Crazy things were going on all over.

On June 13, in Bakersfield, California, Carlotta Fondrin, a pro-life volunteer, was picketing outside an abortion clinic when a car pulled up. A young woman got out, and Carlotta tried to give the man who was driving some literature, but the man cursed her and then pulled a gun on her. Carlotta backed slowly away, scared to death. The man drove off, and Carlotta called the police.

From the information Carlotta supplied, the police quickly identified the man who pulled a gun, and they showed up at his home. The man showed the police the gun, which turned out to be a pellet gun.

He was not arrested.

Tim Palmquist, a pro-life leader in Bakersfield, became furious when he heard that the man who pulled a gun on one of his volunteers was not charged with anything. Pro-lifers were routinely thrown into jail for the craziest infractions, and Tim thought it was blatantly unfair for this man to pull a gun on a pro-lifer and get away with it. The fact that he had shown the police a pellet gun was not enough, in Tim's mind, to erase the seriousness of the charge or to explain the police department's lack of interest.

Tim packed his wife and children into the car and drove to the police station. His request to see the police report was refused because his name wasn't on it, so he changed his tack and argued that the Bakersfield police were applying a double standard. The district attorney in Bakersfield had often stated publicly that pro-lifers should "expect mistreatment" because abortion is such a volatile issue. But Tim wanted to know why *only* the pro-lifers were brought to account, while those supporting abortion could get away with anything.

Tim's wife was shocked when the police officer rushed around the counter, grabbed Tim, threw him facedown on the floor, and slapped handcuffs on him.

"Why are you doing this?" Tim demanded.

"You have a pen in your hand and you were making stabbing motions," the officer responded.

Tim was charged with Assault with a Deadly Weapon on an Officer, Disturbing the Peace, and Resisting Arrest.

This incident, coupled with the earlier seizure of O.R.'s equipment, showed just how far the police were willing to bend the rules to shut Rescue down. In fact, many in the abortion movement (not to mention some sectors of the pro-life movement) went on record saying they had defeated Rescue. It was "dead" and "irrelevant."

Yet it was just a month or so away from its biggest coup.

Two days after Tim was arrested, Flip and I did the NBC *Today* show. The local news interest about our friendship had finally filtered up to NBC's national bureau, resulting in an invitation to the nationally broadcast Saturday morning show.

Flip and I had fun planning our trip to New York. "Miss Norma," Flip said, "I want you to come with me to David Wilkerson's church when we get into New York."

Times Square Church is based in Manhattan and uses the same building in which the rock opera *Jesus Christ Superstar* opened twenty-five years ago. David Wilkerson, of *The Cross and the Switchblade* fame, founded the church in 1987.

I didn't know David Wilkerson from David Bowie, so I thought, *What could it hurt?* But I wasn't about to let Flip off so easily. "Okay, but first, you have to come to my church here in Garland."

I didn't really have a church, of course, but I knew there was one that purported to call itself Christian and that dabbled in the more mystical stuff that I was used to. A lesbian friend of mine had recommended it when I told her I was getting interested in "spiritual stuff" again. I figured if Flip and I were going to go church shopping, he should at least look at one that my friends felt comfortable in.

On that Sunday, I pulled up to a little white country church with some very sweet people and some rather strange ideas and practices. Flip arrived a few minutes later with Jason, one of his teenage sons.

At the end of the service, the pastor called for people to come forward to receive prayer. I watched a middle-aged gentleman go forward, fall to the ground, and start twitching like he was having a cardiac arrest. This was not the relatively mild form of "being slain in the Spirit" that you occasionally see on those late-night religious television shows. Every muscle in this man's body jerked violently in spastic movements.

He's gonna die! I shouted to myself. *He's gonna die, right here in church!* But nobody around him moved. Everybody acted like this was normal, so I suddenly felt abnormal for being so alarmed.

I couldn't take it anymore. "I gotta get out of here," I whispered to Flip, then bolted out the back door.

I didn't stop until I reached a tree that was a block away. It was not enough just to be out of the church; I wanted off the property! At the time, I was addicted to Dean Koontz and Stephen King horror novels, and every plot came sailing back into my mind. I fumbled around in my purse until I could pull out a cigarette and calm down.

What was I doing here? Why was I at a church? Why had I invited Flip Benham, of all people? What was going on with me?

I sucked hard on that cigarette, blotting out the panic that rose within me. I saw Jason walk out of the church and come toward me. "Are you okay, Miss Norma?" he asked.

"Sure, honey," I said. "I just needed a cigarette, that's all."

A few minutes later we were joined by Flip. He smiled and shook his head. "Miss Norma," he said, "this is not what most churches are like." His voice was so calm, so understanding. "Will you come with me to David Wilkerson's church in Times Square?"

"I don't want none of that stuff touching me," I protested, pointing at the church. I knew the spiritual world was real, and I knew it was full of fearful things. I didn't want to go back anytime soon. I was ready to call a halt to this spiritual exploration.

"It won't be anything like that, I assure you," Flip said.

I trusted him. I don't know why, but I trusted him. "All right," I said. "But if anything like that happens . . ."

"It won't," Flip assured me.

Since I had some friends in New York, I got there about a week before the NBC show was scheduled. I began to miss the crazy Christians—Flip, Ronda, and Emily—so on Friday I called NBC and bugged them until they gave me the number where Flip was staying.

He did not seem surprised when I called. I made sure he was okay, and we caught up on each other's week.

The next morning we met in the Green Room, the place where guests await their cue. There was an incredible spread of food waiting for us—danishes, doughnuts, fruits, breads, all kinds of breakfast foods. I could have eaten that stuff all day long.

Flip seemed a little bit unnerved, which surprised me, but finally he said, "Miss Norma, I want you to have this."

I looked up and he held out a brand-new Bible.

"It's the Bible you said you never had, so you can read it whenever you want."

"Thank you, Flip."

Who knows what I would have done with a Bible just a few months before? I'm sure I would have found some creative way to desecrate it, but now I felt grateful. I could sense that my friendship with Flip was deepening.

During the interview, the positive feelings that had been generating between Flip and me died. When we ate together or talked together outside on the bench or even visited a church together, everything was fine, but when Flip started telling the host, "Miss Norma knows she's responsible for thirty-five million deaths," I felt betrayed.

He's my friend, I thought. *He's not supposed to talk about his friend like that.* Whenever he addressed abortion, it was like he became the same Flip Venom I had always known—and hated. It was the same voice, the same body, the same expression, but not the same man. He used fighting words. He called what I was doing sin.

I'll get him on the plane, I said to myself. *He's not getting away with this.* But then I remembered that I had promised to go with him to David Wilkerson's church. I decided to hold my tongue until we got on the return flight home. I would go to David Wilkerson's church. But I was gonna bring some friends with me.

What Happened to the Old Norma?

When church started, I was surprised to find that I actually enjoyed the praise and worship. The whole atmosphere was a new thing for me. I looked at the faces of these Christians and, though I didn't believe as they believed, I envied them for what they had.

When David started preaching, I was even more impressed. He began hammering away at pastors, of all people! Next, he turned to lay Christians who tended to be judgmental.

This is good stuff, I thought.

Then he started talking about homosexuals. I always try to be broad-minded. I do my best to give people the benefit of the doubt. In this instance, however, my patience was stretched, though not because of my own situation. As I mentioned before, I had ended my lesbian relationship with Connie a couple of years earlier. In fact, the reason I had adopted the lesbian lifestyle was in large part because I had experienced so much trouble with men. It should be obvious to any straight-thinking person that most "lesbians" don't experience three problem pregnancies, as I had. But the truth is, I finally got so frustrated with men that I thought, *At least with women, I can't get pregnant.*

I loved it when David beat up on pastors and Christians, but when he started talking about homosexuals, he was talking about my friends. The ones who had come with me got up in the middle of the sermon and walked out. Out of loyalty, I followed them. I had invited them, and I thought I should stay with them.

Flip followed several minutes later and soon got involved in a very heated discussion just outside the church. The funny thing is, I stayed completely out of it. I've never been one to avoid a good fight; I love the smell of conflict—or at least, I used to. It dawned on me that I was not acting like my old self anymore.

My friends noticed a difference as well. I told one of them that I thought she shouldn't be living with her boyfriend since they weren't married. "Aren't you becoming a Miss Goody Two-Shoes?" she answered.

"It's just not right," I said. I wasn't a Christian yet, but God was awakening my conscience.

On the flight back to Dallas, Flip and I sat next to each other. Instead of being angry at Flip, I became worried at his appearance. He looked pale and tired, and that concerned me.

"Are you sure you got enough to eat?" I asked him.

Flip smiled, then laughed. "Miss Norma," he said, "you're nothing but a big mama, a real mother hen. You haven't stopped worrying about me since I set foot in New York."

He was right of course. He had seen right through me. And the irony of Flip Benham, leader of Operation Rescue, extolling Norma McCorvey, Jane Roe of *Roe v. Wade,* for her maternal qualities, did not escape me.

The plane suddenly hit an air pocket of turbulence and jolted sharply. "Oh my goddess!" I shouted out, then looked at Flip and saw his disappointment.

We could get so close, but in many ways, we were still so very far apart.

CHAPTER

20 When Enemies Cooperate

Our growing friendship created a strange cooperation. When I had a problem, I took it up with Flip, and we began working out deals.

On one Saturday, a new set of protesters started showing up one by one, and then two by two. By nine o'clock, there were at least fifty of them, and in our small side street, that was enough to create the feeling of chaos. I didn't recognize a single face, and I was terrified. There was no telling what they might do.

When situations such as this arise, I am an action-oriented person. I prefer any activity over indecision, so I started writing down license plate numbers. If things got ugly, at least the police would have some identifications to follow up on.

But soon there were too many to track down. I felt overwhelmed. Rescue knew we weren't performing abortions during the day in these particular months, because our abortionist was pinch-hitting at a neighboring clinic; procedures at our location were done only during the evening hours. These people knew enough—that we performed abortions—to hurt us. But they obviously did not know enough—that we weren't performing them that morning—to properly understand the situation, and it scared me. I had come to trust that none of the people from

Rescue would hurt me physically, but I didn't trust these people because I didn't know them.

And then, almost like an angel, Flip walked out of the Rescue offices. Who would have guessed, a few months earlier, that I would welcome such a sight? Certainly not me! Yet now I jumped at the opportunity, though I did it in the typical Norma McCorvey style.

"Look," I said, "why don't you call your yahoos and ask them to leave? Their presence is very well known and Arnie isn't here—" meaning, you know we aren't doing any abortions right now "—and we don't need this kind of stuff."

Had I thought about this appeal beforehand, I might never have made it. I was admitting to the leader of the opposition that I felt overwhelmed, and that I didn't know how to cope with this new threat. I was revealing a potential weakness; if Flip had been that kind of man, he could have exploited it.

In short, I had made myself vulnerable, but instead of Flip using that against me, he looked at me with concern, saw my agitation, and said, simply, "Okay." I watched him walk over to the lead protester and say something. He was too far away for me to make out his exact words, but within minutes the protesters peeled off and began to leave.

Flip watched them leave, then turned back and faced me. "You know, Miss Norma," he said, "I used to be pro-choice. In fact, when my wife found out she was pregnant with our twins, I told her to have an abortion."

"You've got to be kidding me!" I said. "What did she say?"

"She told me, 'No, it's my body, and I'll do with my body as I please.'"

I was dumbfounded. His wife had just repeated the abortion movement's most effective spiel—my body, my right, my choice—but she had used it to defend a birth, not an abortion.

"What happened next?" I asked.

"She gave birth to twin boys," Flip answered. "Today, those twins are my best friends. I was one hundred percent wrong in asking her to have an abortion."

The walls defending my abortion stance began to crumble. They didn't sound quite as logical as they had before. Once I realized that pro-lifers weren't monsters—that, in fact, they could even protect me—I was able to accept some of these bits of truth that Flip kept throwing my way.

At the same time, my relationship with the abortion movement had begun to boil.

The Fissure Grows

As I experienced a growing affinity with the Operation Rescue people, I felt a growing distance with my colleagues in the abortion movement. They resented my relationship with Flip—it was yet one more reason for them to attack me. In fact, a nasty E-mail message, written by an abortion activist, was brought to my attention. This E-mail message was sent to a conference full of proabortion women:

> Subject: The Odd Couple
>
> Hi, y'all.
>
> As I sipped my coffee and scanned the newspaper on Saturday, the NBC Today Show host announced that a well known pro-choice activist and her "closest antiabortion friend" would be on after the break. I could hardly wait.
>
> Who were they? None other than Norma (Roe) McCorvey and her pal, Flipper Venom. There she was, cooing about how, on the day they met, Flipper had accused her of being responsible for a gazillion babies' deaths. But, she said, he contacted her later and apologized for hurting her feelings. She sensed he was sincere, and they've been best buds ever since. She indicated that she believes he can help her find the "more spiritual path" she is now seeking. Yech.

> What's next? Recanting her past "sins"?
>
> The clinic where she works is immediately next door to Flipper's office, and antis are allowed one minute to try to persuade patients not to enter the women's clinic. If they are unsuccessful, the women are hassled no more. How charming.

They could laugh all they wanted. That wouldn't stop me. But when I got alone, I had my own questions to answer. Was Flip really for real? Or was he just trying to put one over on me?

I had to find out.

"Why Is He Doing This?"

At first, I didn't understand why Flip was telling me the stories about his past—especially the ones that made him look less than perfect, like encouraging his wife to get an abortion and staying out all night to drink.

I would come home at night and repeat the stories to Connie. "I don't understand why he's telling you all this," she agreed.

If Flip was supposed to be my archenemy, why was he giving me information that could prove damaging to his reputation? What I didn't understand at the time was that he was witnessing to me. By showing me his failures, he was hoping that I might see how God could forgive my own failures.

I didn't realize this because nobody, to my knowledge, had ever witnessed to me before. I guess they thought I was a lost cause, a hopeless case, someone who would only be a waste of time. And if they had asked me, I would have agreed with them.

But for some reason, Flip did not share that opinion. He was one of the few people who did not believe that saving Jane Roe was too big a task even for God.

When my uncertainty about Flip's motives got to be too much, I went to the only place I knew where I could get an answer: I began dealing my tarot cards, which is sort of like playing solitaire in the spirit realm.

"Why is this man being so nice to me and telling me his innermost secrets?" I asked, and then dealt out the cards to find an answer.

I gasped when the answer was signified by the terrifying card of the skeleton, representing death. Beads of cold sweat crawled up my neck, and I became more suspicious than ever. Was Flip softening me up so that he could eventually kill me? That's what the cards were saying!

I need a second opinion, I thought, and pulled out my Ouija board. But then I remembered some frightening experiences with the board and said to myself, *I don't want to know the answer that bad,* and I put the board away.

Next I turned to my crystals, which I often carried in a sack. To read crystals, you throw them out and look at the formation. There's no right or wrong way to objectively read crystals. The answer is whatever you perceive the crystals to be telling you, and in this instance, the answer was ambiguous.

So, I thought, none of my usual methods of guidance were working. The skeleton card had to be a mistake, because whenever I talked to Flip, I felt much better. In fact, at work, I caught myself anxiously glancing out the window to see if his car was there. When I saw it, an unexplainable peace came over me. Somehow, I knew that everything was going to be okay. There was no reason to worry. He might never stop telling me I was a sinner, but he would never kill me.

In contrast to my earlier impressions of Flip, I had come to know him as a man of his word. Whatever he said was the way it was. Whether the news would be good—"Okay, Norma, I'll get the protesters out of here"—or bad—"Norma, what you are doing is an offense to God"—he'd tell me directly, and I respected that.

So, ironically enough, the major threat in my life, according to early media reports, had become my biggest comfort. The terrorists had become bearers of peace—and peace was something I had very little of.

Drawing Closer

My growing relationship with Flip, Ronda, and Emily could not overcome the fact that I was a pretty miserable person. A few years earlier, I had asked the Ouija board if I would die a happy person, and the board said, "No." Nothing in my life—so far—could be used to prove the Ouija board wrong.

This was what I call my "drinking and thinking" stage. I would go to a bar, order a couple of pitchers of beer, and spend an entire evening pondering everything that was going on. My growing relationship with Flip and Ronda, my disenchantment with the abortion movement, my overall sadness. I just sat there, night after night, drinking and thinking, drinking and thinking.

I never found an answer in the bar. Instead, I'd get so tired I would finally be forced to make a phone call (I was in no shape to drive) and ask someone to pick me up, hoping they would engage me in as little conversation as possible.

Emily must have noticed my unhappiness because, soon, my salvation became a major preoccupation with her. I remember the first time she skipped up to me and asked, "Miss Norma, would you go to church with us?"

I didn't have the heart to refuse her, so I played with her a bit. "When are you going to church, honey?"

"Saturday night."

"Emily, nobody goes to church on Saturday night." (That's how little I knew.)

"We do, Miss Norma, and it would be sooo cool if you would go to church with us."

I sighed. "Well, Emily, let's be cool on another night." I didn't want to disappoint her, but I couldn't stomach another church service.

However, as God inched closer into my life, I did begin shedding some of my disbelief. For many years I wore a button that had the word *GOD* on it, with a red slash through it. I kept it near a little bottle of Valium, and one day I saw it and caught myself thinking, *Okay, okay, so you're real.*

There was no reason for me to say this. Nothing momentous had happened. I just suddenly realized that God existed. I could no more deny the fact of his existence than I could pretend that the earth was flat. Of course, I wasn't ready to convert or anything; I just finally admitted that there was a God.

I didn't know it at the time, but this was a major concession. Something momentous was brewing deep within my soul.

That afternoon, without comment, I marched into Flip's office and dropped the button in front of him. He just smiled. I smiled back. We didn't need words. Something much deeper was taking place.

CHAPTER 21 Laughing Flowers

This is where the story starts to get a little weird. If it rested on my testimony alone, I wouldn't expect you to believe it, but several people were involved. Something strange was happening inside our abortion clinic.

As soon as O.R. moved in, you could feel a different spiritual presence. We no longer felt so comfortable in what we were doing, and I would soon live through some of the most frightening and bizarre experiences of my life.

Footsteps

"What's wrong, Connie?" I asked.

It was just a few days after the first "Second Saturday" altercation, and Connie had come into my office looking frightfully white, like she had just seen a ghost. It was past business hours, and we were trying to complete some paperwork, so we were the only two people in the clinic.

"Norma, you'll never believe it, but I just heard something."

"So?"

"It sounded like this—" She thumped her fingers on the table in rapid motion, as if she were signaling impatience.

"I'm sorry? So?" I just didn't get it, and Connie was having a difficult time explaining her fright.

Connie is not an alarmist—she doesn't have an imagination—so I knew to take her fright seriously. I stuck my head out of my office, looked up and down the hall, and didn't see a thing.

Why did Connie find that sound so eerie? Clearly, nobody else was in the office, and since we changed the pass codes every two weeks, security was pretty tight. But Connie knew all this, and she had been alone inside the clinic at night many times before, but never frightened.

What she said next practically made my blood freeze. "To tell you the truth, Norma, it sounded just like a baby running down the hallway."

Panic washed over me like a shower. Something in her words sounded so convincing, it took the strength and courage right out of me. Connie and I clung to each other and began casing the office, going down one hallway and up another, afraid of what we might find. Then we finally ended up outside the door where the procedures were done. I took a deep breath, and we pushed open the door.

There was nothing.

Connie and I relaxed a little bit and finally decided that we must have been playing mind games with each other. Both of us were stressed out over all that was happening with O.R., so maybe we just slipped a little over the edge. We decided to forget about what Connie heard; we didn't give the baby's footsteps a second thought—until the day I heard the flowers laugh.

The Baby's Laugh

A few days later, I was back at the clinic. Following my normal practice, I went outside to gather some flowers for the recovery room. I always liked to make the room look as cheery as possible for the patients. As long as it didn't cost Arnie anything, he was willing to oblige my indulgence.

I went to a bush of wild sunflowers and cut a few blooms. Then I heard a baby's laugh.

"Tee-hee-hee."

I dropped the flowers and slowly backed away, then ran inside the clinic.

Connie saw me come in all out of breath and asked, "Norma, what happened?"

We were all on edge. She thought maybe somebody from O.R. had threatened me.

"I was cutting some flowers, and I heard a baby laugh."

Connie looked at me with a puzzled expression. I could tell she believed me, because she remembered hearing the footsteps; but neither of us had a clue about how to handle this craziness. We had been friends for twenty-six years, and neither one of us had ever started losing our minds.

"Go home, Norma," Connie said. "You look like you've seen living death. You'll scare all the clients away."

"Connie," I protested. "Something is out there. I heard it. We'd better go check."

"Nothing's out there, Norma. Go home."

In Mourning

The next day, I was determined not to lose my mind. Early in the morning, I decided I was going back to the clinic, I was going back to that bush, I was going to cut some more flowers, and I was not going to hear a child's laughter.

As soon as I got to the clinic I went to my desk, picked up my scissors, then went out the back door. I cut some more of the same flowers and was shaken to my marrow when I heard the same "tee-hee-hee."

With a desperate energy, I tore that bush apart. It was a thicket of wild sunflowers, so my arms got pretty scratched up, but I was determined to find that baby.

The only problem was, of course, there was no baby. . . .

Then I did something really strange—at least for me. I looked up into the heavens and said, "Okay, God, I don't know what you're doing up there, but I wish you would stop this. It isn't funny."

I never talked to God. Had no use to. He was sort of the enemy, after all.

So what was I doing talking to him now?

And then a dull sadness came over me. I wasn't panicked anymore, I was just very, very sad, as if I were mourning the death of something precious. It came suddenly and was strong enough to physically hurt my heart. I felt like a really close friend had died, or that many close friends had died—but nobody came to mind. Still, I could not shake the pervasive sadness.

I went back into the clinic and didn't even try to hide the fact that I was crying. It was no use. "I'm going home," I said. "I can't take it anymore."

I sat on the front porch all day. Cars went by, people out for a walk came down the street, an occasional dog barked, but Norma McCorvey barely moved a muscle the rest of that day. She sat in her chair and mourned. If you would have asked her, "What are you mourning?" she could not have told you. But the sadness wouldn't leave.

Connie came home, took one look at me, and said, "Are you okay?"

With a startlingly passive expression, I answered, "I'm fine. I think I'm losing my mind, but I'm okay."

More Footsteps

Connie and I didn't dare tell anyone else about what we had heard in the clinic. From years of practice, we had learned the rules of survival, and that meant never letting down your guard. Suspicion, pettiness, backbiting, and sometimes open hostility ran rampant at the clinic, and the last thing we wanted to do was give other people some ammunition against us.

A few days later, after the clinic had closed Connie and I left to run some errands. Another worker, Lynn, stayed behind, though everybody else was gone. Lynn is a pretty solid girl with a strong personality and a confident sense of assurance. She's certainly not an alarmist, but when we returned from our errands, Lynn stumbled toward us with a ghastly look of fear on her face.

"What's wrong with you, kid?" I asked.

"You wouldn't believe me if I told you."

Connie and I looked at each other.

"Try me," I said.

"I heard children's feet, little children's feet, running up and down the hall, but I couldn't see anything."

"How about that?" I said, looking at Connie.

"See, I knew you wouldn't believe me," Lynn said defiantly.

"What makes you think we don't?" I asked her.

"Well, I don't know, I'm probably just going crazy."

That's all Connie and I needed. Lynn's experience validated our own. "I don't think so," I said.

Strange as it may seem, we didn't talk about it much after that, even with Lynn. We didn't even tell Lynn that we had heard the same thing. It was just too weird, and the easiest way to deal with it was by denying that any of it had happened.

But something inside me had changed.

CHAPTER 22 Falling Toward Life

When do you all kill little babies?"

How would *you* like to handle that call on a Monday morning? Certain I was speaking to a pro-lifer or somebody from Rescue, I let the southern-sounding woman on the other end of the line have it.

"We normally kill little boys on Thursdays," I answered, "little girls on Fridays, and we mix 'em up on Saturdays."

"Well, I want to ask you a question." Her tone of voice surprised me. This was not a crank call after all. The woman was serious.

"Sure. Go ahead."

"Is it really a baby?" She went on to explain to me that her daughter was eighteen weeks pregnant and was considering having an abortion.

This is where the story gets confusing, even for me. Remember, I'm supposed to be acting as a marketing director for an abortion clinic. I'm being paid to sell abortions. But something inside me was breaking, and this is what I said.

"Ma'am, how many children have you had?"

"Three."

"What came out of your body? Were they fish, or were they little human babies?"

"That's preposterous. I had human babies, of course."

"Well, I think you answered your own question," I said.

Then I got really crazy. "Besides, we don't see patients over eighteen weeks here," I added. That was a complete lie. Arnie aborted them all the time. He loved it because the profit was so high.

"Then can you give me the name of a clinic that does?"

"I don't know of any clinic that does abortions that far along." This was another lie—I knew of several clinics that performed late-term abortions.

I hung up the phone and thought, *What am I doing?* It was as if I was watching myself as an objective observer rather than as an active participant. We made a lot of money on late-term abortions, and I had just let one go!

Connie charged into my office. "Man, I've had it!"

"What?"

"This witch just called me and asked me when we were killing little baby boys and girls, and you know what I said?"

"What?"

"I said Thursday, Friday, and Saturday!"

I was startled that her call was so similar to mine. "Well, you know what I just said?"

"What?"

"I just told a woman that it was a real baby."

"Well, good for you," Connie said. She walked out, then rushed right back in. "You said *what*?"

"A woman's daughter was eighteen weeks pregnant, and I told her it was a real baby and that we didn't perform abortions that far along."

"Norma," Connie said, looking me in the face, "we're losing it."

I laughed.

"Maybe so, Connie, but you know what? I don't even feel bad about it. Let's see how far we can take this thing."

We were going to have a little fun.

In the next weeks, Connie and I began sabotaging our own clinic's business. Our frustration with Arnie had reached a fevered pitch. A frequent phone conversation would go like this:

"A Choice for Women, this is Norma, may I help you?"

"I need to come in and see your doctor."

"What for, honey? Do you want a pap smear?"

"No."

"Do you want a breast exam?"

"No."

I'd make them go through every option until they finally said, "I want one of those abortions."

"Oh, okay, let me order you one right here." I then took my mouth away from the phone as if I was shouting out an order for a burger and fries and yelled, "Give me one abortion going!"

The women on the other end would usually remain unperturbed. The conversation was so odd, they just ignored it. "Well, how much is it gonna cost me?"

"That depends," I'd say. "How much do you want to pay to kill your baby?"

"They said it wasn't a baby."

"Who is 'they'? What do you think is inside you, a fish?"

We were cruel, very cruel. It was our way of waking up to the truth of what we had been doing for so many years; the emotional and spiritual upheaval were so great, we did things I'm not at all proud of. By this time, I think Connie and I both knew that what we were doing was wrong, but we didn't know how to make things right—so we indirectly attacked abortion by running off business.

Almost immediately, business at A Choice for Women took a nosedive. Before O.R. moved in, we averaged about thirty-five abortion patients a weekend. By the time I left, we were down to nine or fewer.

Arnie became furious. "Norma," he asked me, "how come we no have patients?"

I didn't hide a thing. In fact, I flaunted it. "Because," I told him, "I tell the women we aren't killing little babies on Wednesday; they have to come in Thursday through Saturday to do it."

Arnie was too afraid of confrontation to stand up even to this with anything more than words. "Norma," he said, "you must not say that!"

"Yeah, well, what are you going to do about it?"

I had some very antagonistic feelings by this time. For starters, I knew exactly what we charged for each abortion: starting at $295 for abortions performed around 6–11 weeks; $395 for 12–13 weeks; $495 for 14–15 weeks; $695 for 16–17 weeks; $795 for 18–19 weeks; all the way up to $1,200 for even later abortions.

And for bringing all these abortions in, I got paid six dollars an hour.

Don't think for a minute that doctors who are looking at these figures will put just anybody on the phone. I was good. My job was to make the appointment and to get the women to show up, and I had an enviable 90 percent show-up rate—until, that is, I started intentionally sending people away.

I still wasn't a true believer, however. "Give me a raise, and I'll bring 'em all back," I told Arnie. "I'll make it all right." My conscience was pricked, but I could still be bought.

"No, I pay you enough now."

Fine, I thought. *Then you bring them back.*

Referring for Life

To make matters worse, I also started referring women next door—to Operation Rescue!

"A Choice for Women, this is Norma."

"I need to get an abortion." The quivering voice on the other end of the line alerted me to the fact that I wasn't talking to a woman. This was a girl.

"How old are you, honey?"

"Fifteen."

"Girl, does your mama know what you're doing?"

"No. If she found out, she'd go crazy. She'd kill me."

"I don't believe that. Let me give you the phone number of some people who will take care of you."

Operation Rescue handled these referrals perfectly. If they had made a big deal about it, gone to the press, and proclaimed their victory, that would have been the end of it. My fighting pride would have taken over, and my process of conversion would have ground to a halt—of that I'm sure.

Instead of grandstanding, however, O.R. treated my behavior as the most natural thing in the world. "Sure, Miss Norma, we'd love to talk to her. Send her over."

There was no triumphant condescension in their tone of voice, no claiming of victory, just a pleasant agreement to help a friend. We were supposed to be enemies, but, somehow, we had begun to act like allies.

A Living Sticker

A few weeks later, Ronda told me she was going to look for furniture for the crisis pregnancy center. "I know the store you need to look at," I said, and we set a date to go shopping for furniture together.

I'm sure no one was more surprised than Ronda that Jane Roe would offer to help her furnish the crisis pregnancy center. Ronda, in fact, was scared even thinking about it, so she asked several women from her church to pray for her.

Ronda was not the only one who was scared. We had agreed that Ronda would pick me up, which meant that Ronda would find out where I lived. After you've had your house shot up, you're a little particular about who gets ahold of your address. Was I willing to trust one of O.R.'s leaders with that sensitive piece of information?

"Ronda," I warned her, "if I tell you where I live, you must promise me that you'll never, ever tell anyone else how to get there."

"I promise," Ronda said.

"Ronda Mackey," I said again, wanting to emphasize how important this was to me, "as I live and breathe, if I wake up some morning and find rescuers demonstrating outside my window, I'll, I'll, I'll . . . I'll have a conniption fit."

I know, it sounds funny to say "conniption fit," but I didn't know how to express myself very well without curse words. For me, it was an entirely new experience to make a threat without throwing in a few choice obscenities, and conniption fit was the only thing that came to mind!

"That includes Flip," I added. "I don't want Flip to know. Will you promise me that?"

"Yes," Ronda said.

I gave her my address, hoping that I was not making a tragic mistake.

The day of our adventure, Ronda and her two girls picked me up. I needed to get some money for lunch, so I looked at Ronda and said, "Hey Ronda, would you mind pulling over to that convenience store? I need to cash in a bunch of scratched-off lotto tickets."

Ronda laughed, rolled her eyes, and pulled over. Throughout our early friendship, there were these constant reminders of our different values.

Fifteen minutes later, we pulled up to Chili's for lunch. We slid into a booth, with Ronda and Chelsey occupying one side, and Emily sliding in next to me on the opposite side. Emily was all over me, hugging me, smiling into my eyes, hanging on to my arm. Ronda started fidgeting; something was clearly making her uncomfortable.

"You know, Norma," Ronda finally said after a big sigh, "Emily was almost aborted." And there she told me her story. She didn't make the connection—"and it's your fault"—but she didn't have to. This precious girl, throwing more love my way than anybody had in years, was almost never born because of an affidavit I had signed.

I was somber as we left the restaurant, but did my best to keep a brave face. When we pulled up to the furniture store, we saw two winged-back chairs in the window. "Those would be perfect," I shouted, and Ronda agreed.

"They do look nice," she said. "Let's go in and get a closer look."

I jumped out of the car with the eagerness that comes only from shopping. We looked at the chairs for a while and walked around the store, then I excused myself to go outside and smoke a cigarette.

As soon as I walked out of the store, I caught a glimpse of Ronda's van and almost collapsed on the spot.

Because Ronda routinely parked her van in the parking lot where our abortion clinic was located, she made sure she kept clean, visible bumper stickers on it at all times. That way, women would be given the opportunity to consider a pro-life slogan before they came inside our clinic. For some reason, I had never noticed these stickers on Ronda's van before, but suddenly, one of them hit me between the eyes:

Abortion Stops a Beating Heart

The vivid red in the sticker just about knocked me over. The heart pictured on it looked so real, I wouldn't have been surprised if it had started beating right in front of my eyes. Spiritually, I was crushed.

At that same moment, Ronda and the girls came out of the store, and I saw Emily skipping behind Ronda. The thought that Emily's heart might have been intentionally stopped overwhelmed me. I couldn't take it.

And then when I realized that I had signed the affidavit that resulted in the law being changed so that Ronda could have legally stopped Emily's heart, I was practically overcome with grief, horror, and revulsion.

My whole body hurt just thinking about it.

And then, I don't know if it was a vision or what, I saw Emily not as a young girl, but as a tiny, aborted infant—but an infant that bore Emily's unmistakable features. It was just a flash of a vision, over before I knew it had started, but the sadness it left behind was overwhelming.

Five minutes earlier, Ronda, the girls, and I had been laughing like silly schoolchildren. Suddenly, I was as morbid and downcast as someone who had just been told they had less than twenty-four hours left to live.

Ronda instantly sensed that something was wrong.

"You just have to take me home," I told Ronda. "I can't deal with this." I put on my sunglasses so Emily and Chelsey couldn't see the tears welling up in my eyes.

What happened?

It was the first time abortion had been personalized for me. I no longer saw abortion as a convenient way of dealing with "products of conception" or "missed periods." Instead, abortion represented the "legal right" to end the life of a child as precious as Emily. *This beautiful young girl could have been legally killed without penalty,* I thought—and it was all my fault.

The heaviness that covered me was suffocating. The bumper sticker haunted me. I sat silently in the passenger's seat, asking myself, *How can I love this lady and her two children and still be pro-choice? I'll lose her!* But I didn't want to lose her! This was the woman I had trusted with my address, the woman who in turn had trusted me with her firstborn child.

I jumped out of the van as soon as Ronda dropped me off. Talking was an impossibility, given my emotional state. As soon as I got inside the house, I spent a good hour crying, then Ronda and I talked on the phone for over an hour later in the day.

It was around this time that Ronda says she finally began to get over her picture of me as the symbol of legalized abortion. My weakness, of which I was desperately ashamed, made me seem more human to Ronda. And my delight in her children caught her totally by surprise. I was the last person she expected to take an interest in little kids.

"She's Ready"

Now that Ronda saw me as a real person, we began relating on an entirely new level. In June 1995 Ronda's husband, Ron, who works for a major computer-related firm, found out I was still trying to operate my home computer using DOS, so he purchased Microsoft Windows software and gave it to me.

After years of struggling with outdated software, I thought I was in heaven. I wrote him a card saying, "Dearest Ron, thank you for opening my world up with windows! Plus you have a lovely family. God bless, Norma the storm."

What was this "God bless" all about, I thought, as I reread my own writing. Oh, well. It was in ink, and I was not about to purchase a new card.

I kept calling Operation Rescue for prayer, more frequently now. In early July I had a particularly intense encounter with Flip. Unknown to me at the time, he hung up the phone and looked at Ronda.

"Miss Norma is ready to receive the Lord," he said.

"You're kidding!"

"No. She would have done it right there if I had pushed it."

"Then why didn't you? She needs the Lord!"

"Because I don't think I'm the one who is supposed to do it. I think God has somebody else in mind."

"I wonder who?" Ronda said.

Saved!

"Miss Norma, why don't you go to church with us tonight?"

I don't know how many times Emily had assaulted me with that question. It was hard for me to say no to Emily, so I had always found a way to put her off, but this time I must have been feeling weak. For the first time, I was going to make a promise.

"I can't tonight, honey," I replied, "but I'll go with you next week."

Emily let out a whoop, and I thought she was going to get out of her seat belt right there and begin dancing. I also realized that she was going to hold me to my word. I had thought that by putting off the commitment for a week or so, she might forget; but it was clear to me now that that would never happen. Emily would be counting down the days.

I helped Emily out of the truck and carried her into O.R.'s offices. I "carried" Emily because she was very small for her seven years. People had a tendency to underestimate how smart she was because she looked so much younger. I didn't.

Ronda stood up and walked toward us.

"Here's your firstborn!" I said, handing Emily over to her mom. Ronda looked at Emily and smiled.

"Emily asked me to go to church with you all," I explained.

"She did?" Ronda asked. I could tell she was skeptical.

"Yeah. I can't go tonight, but I thought that maybe I could go next Saturday."

"Well, next Saturday we'll be in Little Rock. We have a big event going on there. What about the week after that?"

"Sure," I said, but I could tell that Ronda was still skeptical. She had this look that said, "The sun's gonna come up a hundred thousand more times before you get to church once!"

It was a long week while Ronda, Flip, and the others were in Little Rock. I actually missed my terrorist friends!

I made sure I was in the office on the Monday that they were due to return, and as soon as I saw Ronda's van pull up, I walked out to greet them.

"I missed you all," I said. I had a huge smile on my face, and I think my sincerity surprised even as it delighted them.

"Well, we missed you, too, Miss Norma," several of them said.

I asked Ronda, "So, when are you going to pick me up for church this Saturday?"

"Well, we can pick you up at five o'clock and go get dinner first."

That night, Ronda called her pastor, Rev. Morris Sheats, and asked him what his sermon was going to be about. He told her something that wasn't very evangelistic so Ronda explained that she was bringing me to church and hoped he'd find a way to include an evangelistic altar call.

"I'm pleased Norma's coming," Pastor Sheats said. "The Holy Spirit will show up, so don't worry—there will be an opportunity for Norma to come to know Christ."

I guess I didn't really have a chance. When the Holy Spirit and Pastor Sheats get together—watch out!

The next day, I did something totally out of character for me. You wouldn't think this would be out of character for most women, but then again, I wasn't your average woman.

I went shopping.

I needed something to wear to church, so I drove over to the mall, looking nervously up at the sky as I walked in, certain that the mere thought of Norma McCorvey, Jane Roe of *Roe v. Wade,* buying clothes so she could look presentable in church, would be enough to call fire out of the sky.

But none of that happened. I found some appropriate clothes. I made it through the week. And on Saturday evening, the Mackey family picked me up about an hour and a half early so that we could go out for dinner.

As we ate, I eagerly told Ronda about my idea for the next great American novel. It was a science-fiction, New Age–type thriller, where people with super vision and enlightened insight ended up saving planet Earth.

Ronda and her husband listened politely, praying that I'd be pointed to an entirely different type of Savior.

Dinner was over—too soon, I thought, as my stomach suddenly felt nervous—and Ronda said we needed to leave to get to church on time.

Suddenly, the word *church* sounded so threatening I could barely contain myself. I was fidgeting during the entire (though relatively short) drive to the church building, feeling not unlike a woman being driven to her execution. As we parked the car, I looked up at Hillcrest Church and wondered what in the world I was doing there.

I cast another worried glance around me. The skies had remained silent, but surely the ceiling and walls would cave in as soon as God realized that Norma McCorvey had dared to set foot in a holy house of worship.

We sat down in chairs. *Okay, when is the ceiling coming down?* I thought. *When will the walls start to crumble? The glass is going to start shooting out any second now. I just know it.*

I thought I stuck out like a big red thumb, as if I were the only new person there. What was I supposed to do next? Several offering envelopes were tucked into the bulletin that was given to me, so I messed around in my purse until I came up with two dollars.

I really had no idea what to expect. Part of me thought that Flip would come bursting onto the stage, replete with lasers and surround sound, and bark out my damnation. Flip didn't even attend this church, but I didn't know that then. I just assumed that everybody at Rescue always hung out together.

I expected any of a hundred things to happen, just not the thing that really did happen.

Though I assumed I was a stranger in this church, half of the congregation knew who I was—they had been warned ahead of time—and they were praying their hearts out. Ronda had called her growth group (a home fellowship group), and then called the leader of every other growth group she could think of. People all over the congregation were praying for me. Ronda's husband, Ron, who sat next to us, doesn't remember a word of the sermon. He was too busy pleading with God for me to accept Jesus into my heart.

As the pastor spoke, his words burned their way into my soul. I can't really recall much of what he shared, but each word began to open the window in my heart just a little bit farther. This was truth. This was the way out I had been looking for all my life. I wanted someone to love me. I wanted someone to take care of me. I wanted someone who could wipe out all the ghastly things that I had done and that had been done to me. In an instant, I realized that Jesus Christ was the only one who could do that.

By the time Pastor Sheats got to the ending, when he read John 3:16, I felt my heart pounding.

"For God so loved the world," he read, "that He gave His only begotten Son, that whoever believes in Him should not perish but have everlasting life."

The pastor then told everyone to bow their heads and close their eyes. I started to get really hot. I was even sweating, something this Texas girl rarely does.

"Is anyone here tired of living a sinner's life?" he asked.

How could I say no? I had been tired of it for years, but it was the only life I knew.

I slowly raised my hand. I opened my eyes and looked up to see if that really was my hand raised up high. It was. I couldn't believe it.

"Then I want you to come up to the altar and meet Jesus."

Meet Jesus? I thought. *Did that man say I could go forward and meet Jesus?* Time seemed to stop.

This will be a kick. I've never met Jesus before. My heart started to pound, and I thought, *If I get up the nerve to go up front, Jesus had better be there.*

My eyes filled with tears. Ronda noticed my fidgeting and asked me, "Do you want to go up front?"

"Yes," I said.

Ronda was radiantly happy, but I got the distinct impression that she was even more scared than I was. We clasped hands, and I leaned on her for strength, feeling weaker and weaker with each step. Something was happening inside me.

What are you doing??? I asked myself. I then found myself answering my own question. *I'm going to meet Jesus.*

Don't be silly, a voice said. *Jesus isn't up there.*

Oh yes, he is, I thought. *The pastor said so.*

When Ronda and I finally made it to the front, I lifted my head, took one look in Pastor Morris Sheats's eyes, and I saw Jesus. I saw the Spirit of God. It was true. Jesus was meeting me through this man.

How can I describe what happened next? The best way I can explain it is that I felt something "swooshy" inside, like something flew right through me. I began bawling like a baby. I couldn't have held back the tears even if I'd wanted to.

Seeing Jesus in Pastor Sheats's eyes made me feel so incredibly sorry for all my sins, especially for my role in legalizing abortion. As a church counselor led me into the prayer chapel, I was telling myself, *Okay, Norma, this is your judgment day.* In that room I repented of everything I've ever done.

"I just want to undo all the evil I've done in this world," I kept repeating over and over, wringing my hands. "I'm so sorry. I'm so, so sorry. As far as abortion is concerned, I just want to undo it. I want it all to just go away."

Nobody led me in these prayers. The words simply erupted from inside me and forced their way out. I was incredibly sorry. In many ways, it was a supernatural sorrow, and it filled my soul.

A prayer counselor kept praying over me. I vaguely sensed Ronda's presence. The world of the Spirit was more real to me than anything else. I kept getting extremely hot, then extremely cold. One minute, I was shaking the sweat off; the next, I was unbearably chilled, looking for a coat.

"Hold me," I asked Ronda at one point, "I'm cold." It was a hundred degrees out that day, but I was cold.

Finally—I don't know how long it took—I stopped crying. I looked up and saw an altar in front of the chapel's stained-glass windows and an almost instant peace told me that everything was going to be okay. Instead of weeping, I struggled against an uncontrollable, ear-to-ear smile. Not only had the ceiling and walls not caved in, but I no longer felt the pressure of my sin pushing down on my shoulders. The release was so quick, I felt as if I could almost float.

And then it dawned on me. Norma McCorvey, a.k.a. Jane Roe of *Roe v. Wade*, had just become a Christian.

A New Woman

Ron and the girls were waiting for us outside. Emily, of course, was deliriously happy, so we spent the drive home being silly girls—playing pat-a-cake, laughing, just silly stuff.

"Are you going to call Flip and tell him?" I asked Ronda.

"Absolutely not," Ronda said. "He won't believe this hearing it from me. *You* call him."

When Ron pulled up to my house, I realized that an entirely new woman was about to walk through those old, familiar doors. I had almost been killed in this house. I had cried buckets of tears, drunk gallons of alcohol, and consumed obscene quantities of drugs within these walls. This old house had seen everything. But now, it was going to shelter a new woman. I had the same face, but I wore a radically different expression. I had the same past, but I couldn't help smiling as I realized I faced a radically different future.

Connie saw me walk in and politely asked, "How was church?"

"Fine," I said. "By the way, I just accepted Jesus into my heart."

"Well, good. Want a beer?" There was a confused pause, then a wild, "You did *what*?"

I laughed, and Connie laughed. She had spent many an evening trying to get me to convert to Roman Catholicism and I had steadfastly refused to listen. I had even forbade her from hanging any religious art in the house. I couldn't stand the eyes, certain that they would always be looking at me in judgment. So Connie was actually delighted, though clearly surprised.

We chatted for a few minutes until I remembered some important business. "Listen, Connie," I said, "hold that thought. I've got to call Flip."

As soon as Flip answered the phone, I played a little coy. "Well, I went to church tonight," I said.

"Good," Flip answered.

"And I accepted Jesus into my heart."

"Do you mind if I call Ronda?" He wanted to double-check my story and get all the details. I laughed and said that would be fine.

Joy flooded the voice of the man who had once pronounced God's judgment on my soul. He was delighted and did not act as surprised as I expected him to be. Because of his own past, Flip knew how God could call even those people who have fallen far away.

I hung up the phone and marveled at what had taken place. Finally, I had found a love that was all-encompassing. On many occasions, Sarah Weddington had made it clear that to her I was nothing more than a name in a class-action lawsuit. Jane Roe was all that mattered to Sarah; the real Norma McCorvey was irrelevant.

In Jesus, I realized it was exactly the opposite. God did not view me solely through the lens of what I had done or how I had been used. Now, after I had been forgiven, Jane Roe was irrelevant. The woman he loved—the woman he saved—was Norma Leah McCorvey.

CHAPTER

23

A Change of Address

Of course, now that I had become a Christian, working at the clinic seemed impossible. In the first few moments of my conversion, the thought of abortion was not a factor at all. I realized I needed God. That need, and that need alone, consumed me. But once the decision was made, I was overcome by the offensiveness of my abortion-related activities.

On Monday, I wrote out my resignation:

> Dear doctor,
>
> I've become a Christian so I can't work here anymore. This is my official two-weeks' notice.
>
> Norma McCorvey

I handed the note to Connie, since she was technically my superior. She read it and said, "Well, why don't you just go right now?" There was no animosity in her tone; she simply realized I didn't want to be there anymore so she would not try to force me to stay.

I handed Connie my keys, walked right out of the clinic and straight into O.R.'s doors, where I was greeted with a tremendous welcome.

"Helloooo, Miss Norma!" Flip said, giving me a giant bear hug.

"Yeaaa!" Ronda called out.

"I'm ready to go to work," I said.

It was weird sitting on the other side of the wall, yet it was sort of like coming home. Of course, in the world's eyes, this would have been big, big news: Jane Roe turning in her abortion clinic keys and walking next door to Rescue. But Connie was not about to call the press, and I wasn't planning on calling them, either. We decided to keep things quiet for a while so I could get used to what it was like being a Christian.

Flip was sensitive to what had happened to many celebrities who had become Christians, so he and Ronda were both cautious. The memory of one celebrity in particular haunted Flip. About the same time the coffeemaker salesman had walked into Flip's saloon, B. J. Thomas announced that he had become a Christian.

Flip was ecstatic. He loved B. J.'s music and was excited that now he could listen to that voice sing about Jesus. A few years later, however, as Flip entered seminary, he watched with alarm as Thomas started slipping farther and farther away from the faith, until he eventually told a reporter that he was back to believing in reincarnation.

"We've seen enough famous people become Christians and fly up like a rocket only to fall back down like a rock," Flip warned me. "We don't want that to happen to you."

That was fine by me. I had plenty to get used to. My past was inextricably tied up with *Roe v. Wade* and my identity was built largely around my role as the plaintiff. I worked, volunteered, and spent most of my time promoting the legal-abortion movement. I had even been quoted (accurately) in a newspaper saying, "This issue is the only thing I live for. I live, eat, breathe, think everything about abortion."

Overnight, all that had changed, and God and I had a lot of talking to do to set things straight. All my old acquaintances were wrapped up in the abortion movement, so I learned what I could from my new friends at Rescue and Hillcrest (the church where I was saved), and spent many an afternoon talking to God.

At first, it was very awkward for me to talk to God. It started out like this: "Well, God, this is Norma McCorvey."

Silence.

"I'm in Dallas, Texas."

More silence.

What am I supposed to say next? I wondered. I remembered Flip telling me that I could talk to God just like I would talk to a friend, so I decided to give that a try.

"Well, you know, God," I began, "I used to be pro-choice, and I signed this affidavit a long time ago—you were probably too busy to notice—but because of it, abortion became legal in this country. I got involved in all this proabortion stuff, and I know it was the wrong thing to do. I was just scared, and back then, I didn't know how to get in touch with you. I didn't know your phone number, and nobody took the time to tell me how to pray.

"I've done some other wrong things too. I know abortion is a sin. I know my physical relationship with Connie was wrong. And, of course, the drugs. I don't suppose you liked that too much, either."

Even though Connie and I had realized in 1992 that all physical intimacy in our relationship was over, I still felt I needed to set the record straight.

I began reading the Bible all day long. Once I warmed up to praying, I pelted God with so many prayers that I apologized to him at the end of the day. "God, I'm sorry for bothering you so much. You must be really tired by the end of the day, with me blathering along, always trying to get your attention."

I was just afraid that God would grow tired of me.

One day I plopped down in front of Flip's desk and said, "Flip, I'm so worried about God."

Flip smiled. "You're worried about God?" he asked. "Why?"

"I'm sure he's not getting any rest. I can't quit asking him questions. Another one just pops into my mind, and there I am, bothering him again."

"You really are a mother hen, aren't you, Miss Norma?" Flip smiled. "Now you're trying to be a mother hen to God!"

Setting Things Right

I not only wanted to discuss things with God, but I wanted to set them right, as much as I was able to.

"God, I've said some pretty awful things about you," I confessed. "I didn't really mean them. I'm sorry."

And then I thought about all the people I had attacked. I began calling them up, one by one, to ask for their forgiveness. First on my list was Randall Terry, the founder of Operation Rescue. If you've ever met Randy, you know he's one of the most delightful fellows around. He's funny, insightful, and very thoughtful of others. But I had said some mean and nasty things about him without even really knowing who he was.

He was quick to say, "Miss Norma, I forgive you; but thank you for calling and telling me you're sorry."

When I thought about apologizing to Flip, I remembered the Tom Snyder show in particular. After O.R. had moved next door to us, Tom invited me on for an interview, and I said some very cruel things about Flip. I realized I was going to have to take a tape of the interview to Flip as my confession.

I was deathly afraid to do this. Flip had become a close friend, and I did not want to alienate him, especially now. On the other hand, I thought it would be worse if our friendship continued to build and he found out about the tape later. *Better to make a clean slate now,* I thought.

I took the tape over to Flip and said he needed to watch it. "I've got to let you know what I've said about you so that you know exactly what I'm asking for when I ask you to forgive me. You're probably going to hate me. You're probably never going to want to speak to me again, but here it is."

Flip watched it, hugged me, and offered his full forgiveness.

For many weeks, I lived with a continual desire to purge my past, to ask and seek forgiveness, and to make restitution wherever possible. Each day I woke up with my spirit feeling a little lighter than the day before.

A New Family

One of the things that surprised me most about becoming a Christian was the attitude of those I now worked with on a daily basis. At first, I couldn't believe how weird the rescuers were. It was one thing to visit them occasionally while I was working at the clinic. Then I had plenty of suspicions that they were weird.

Now I was absolutely certain they were weird.

Why?

They were always so positive. I would come in all sad and down in the dumps, and they would be enthusiastic and happy and optimistic. Even when I messed up—slipping with a cuss word or something like that—they would look shocked, then encourage me to keep growing. Never did they put me down or expect me to become a different person. They accepted me just the way I was.

It took me a full six months to realize that that's simply the way people are when they know Jesus. No matter how difficult life can be, with Jesus you always have a reason to be optimistic.

It might sound funny to someone who has been a Christian for a long time, but to me this was an entirely new outlook on life. At the clinic, if we weren't getting high (escaping the present) or making crude jokes (escaping the past), we were making plans to do one or the other (escaping the future).

What startled me so much about the Christians at church and at Rescue was how their attitudes were exactly the opposite of what I expected. In the abortion movement, we always assumed that Christians were mean-spirited, judgmental, pleasure-hating radicals. If they opened their mouths at all, we thought, it was only to condemn sinners and deliver a sermon about the wages of wickedness.

In fact, I found out that *we* were the ones who were mean-spirited, self-righteous, and judgmental. It was those in the abortion movement who were ruled by hatred and spite. My entire frame of reference had changed.

Two weeks later, my conversion would become public knowledge—and then I would find out just how hot that hatred could run.

CHAPTER 24

Baptized

My baptism almost never happened.

I thought that by accepting Christ I had put Jane Roe to death forever. Though God had forgiven me, I soon found out that the world would not let me forget.

When Ronda and the folks at Hillcrest Church mentioned that my first step in faith should be baptism, I readily agreed to participate, asking Flip to do the honors. There was just one problem, I told Ronda.

"What's that?" she asked.

"I've never been to a baptism. I don't have a clue about what I should wear."

We talked about a few possibilities, then Ronda broached a sensitive topic. "You don't wear a bra, do you, Norma?"

"Ronda, I haven't owned one of those for thirty years."

"Well, make sure you wear a T-shirt underneath your other shirt. You're gonna be dumped in the water and brought back up, and you don't want anything—"

"I get it, Ronda," I laughingly said.

This was going to be an entirely new life, for sure!

Thank God, news of my conversion had still not been leaked. We knew that eventually people would find out, however, so we decided to do a preemptive strike and let ABC cover the baptism exclusively. Our desire was to contain the media frenzy as much as possible. We trusted Peggy Wehmeyer at ABC, and Flip knew a photographer he trusted from the *Dallas Morning News*. They and their crews would be the only media people notified ahead of time. To both Peggy and the photographer we made explicitly clear our desire to keep this event quiet. They were eager to oblige, and for good reason: they wanted to protect their scoop.

On the day of the baptism, I got up and had my usual cup of coffee. Then I did something I had not done in years. At Ronda's encouragement, I shaved my legs.

Boy, things really had changed!

I got dressed—with a T-shirt underneath—and went to Flip's office. We discussed some of the questions he would ask me at the baptism: "Who is the Lord?" "Do you believe the holy Scriptures of the Old Testament and New Testament to be God's inspired words?" "Do you renounce the devil and his works, and the sinful desires of the flesh, so that you will not follow or be led by them—God granting you mercy and grace?" And then he said, "All right, Miss Norma, the next time I see you will be at the baptism."

This was the calm before the storm.

Reaction

"Norma, did you know Peggy is planning on interviewing some pro-choice people for the ABC piece?"

Ronda's words ignited a white-hot fire inside me. I had agreed to allow Peggy Wehmeyer to cover the baptism, but it was understood that she would be the only correspondent allowed in. Peggy is a Christian, so I trusted her, but I was infuriated when Ronda told me that she had overheard ABC planning on soliciting comments from the pro-choice community. As far as I was concerned, my conversion and my baptism had absolutely nothing to do with my former life as Jane Roe.

"This is not about abortion," I protested to Ronda. "This is about my salvation. It's about the fact that God has come into my life. Who cares what Kate Michelman or Patricia Ireland thinks about my conversion? Their comments aren't relevant!"

I got angrier the more I thought about it. "If Peggy does this, tell her to forget about it, I'm not gonna be baptized."

My conversion was not a publicity stunt. I wanted the baptism to be private. It was a personal decision I had made. I was not ashamed of it, but I did not want it to be reduced to a news item, either.

I had felt this sense of invasion earlier in the week. Peggy was with us when we were at Lee Park, a site of many proabortion demonstrations, doing some background filming for the news item that would run later in the week. While there, I felt drawn to pray. This had been the scene where I had publicly stood up for legalized abortion, and something within me was compelled to now pray to the Author of life.

I walked off by myself to get some privacy, and there I shared some personal thoughts with God. When I came back to rejoin the group, Peggy told me, "Oh, Norma, we heard you praying over there. It was wonderful. We might want to use you praying."

I had forgotten that I was still wearing a microphone. They had heard every word! *What an invasion of privacy,* I thought.

That memory still fresh in my mind, I finally decided that enough was enough. "Just tell Peggy and Flip to forget about it," I said finally. "I'm not being baptized."

If dropping the baptism entirely was the only way to duck the spotlight, so be it. I wasn't saying no to God. I still considered myself a Christian. But I was not about to let my baptism become a heated debate on *Nightline.*

Ronda conveyed the message to Peggy and Flip, and Peggy immediately asked the pointed question: "Well, who told her I was going to talk to the others?"

"I did," Ronda admitted.

"Why did you do that?"

"Because I don't want Norma to go back and watch the news tonight and think that we used her to get a big story." Ronda was very sensitive about using me. She felt the proabortion movement had done precisely that, bringing me forward when it suited them, then casting me aside when it didn't. She was determined I would not experience the same thing from prolifers.

I was touched that Ronda was willing to go to such lengths to protect me and to be absolutely honest with me.

This day was not political. Jane Roe was irrelevant. I trusted Peggy; I knew she was probably getting a lot of pressure from Peter Jennings and the folks at ABC, but I still did not want to participate if the ground rules had changed; and I felt they had.

We had discussed this at great lengths—how to keep the focus on the spiritual, not the political; how to keep the focus on Norma McCorvey, new Christian, not Jane Roe, abortion plaintiff. If the ground rules had changed, I wasn't playing.

Ronda, Flip, and Peggy began praying for me and for God's will to be done.

The Go-Ahead

Meanwhile, I was with Connie at the abortion clinic, refusing to talk to anybody from Rescue. I knew enough about my anger not to take it for granted, and I thought the best thing was to hold off speaking directly to anyone until I got over being angry. Otherwise, I might say something I would later regret.

I left a message on O.R.'s machine. "I'm definitely not being baptized. I thought you said we could trust these people, but obviously, we can't. They've shown their jaundiced faces, and there's no way I'm going to participate."

Ronda called the abortion clinic, and Connie answered the phone. "She really wants to talk to you," Connie said. Connie has this expression that tells me when I'm being completely unreasonable, and she was wearing it then.

"All right," I said. "Tell her to come over."

Ronda walked over and found me pacing inside the reception area. I thought I had left Jane Roe behind. I thought she had been buried in Christ. But now I realized the media would never let me forget her. When I die, the obituaries will almost surely say, "Norma McCorvey, the original plaintiff called Jane Roe in the 1973 Supreme Court Case, *Roe v. Wade* . . ."

But Ronda's gentle words soothed me. I came to realize that I should not let the media keep me from doing something that the Bible called me to do. I could not control how they would report it, but that was really a side issue. For me, the most important thing was that I was doing this for God.

And before God, I was not Jane Roe. When I see God face-to-face, he is not going to remind me of my role in the legalization of abortion. He is simply going to take me into his arms and call me his little girl.

I finally agreed to talk with Flip and Peggy, and Peggy assured me, "We understand this is not a pro-choice, pro-life issue here, but everyone wants to hear what the other side has to say. It will be really short, and we won't let them tear you apart."

I still didn't like it, but when I looked at Flip, I knew I was going to do it. "We've invited an awful lot of people, Miss Norma," he said gently.

I was convicted. Besides, I figured it was too late to back out now, so we decided to go ahead with the baptism.

Connie and I followed Ronda over to the baptism, which would take place in the swimming pool of a Rescue supporter. This was not an easy trip for Connie. She was still working at the clinic at this point, so there were a number of unresolved issues between us. To make matters worse, as Connie diligently followed Ronda's minivan, she could not miss the bumper stickers:

"Abortion Stops a Beating Heart"
"Abortion doesn't make you unpregnant—
It makes you the mother of a dead baby."

Connie looked at me and asked, "Does she really believe that?"

"Yes," I said. "She really believes it." *And now,* I was thinking, *so do I.*

I was impressed as we drove through the Dallas suburbs on our way to the house where the baptism would be held. Ronda stopped in front of a beautiful home.

"I guess we're here," Connie said, looking at me with a funny expression. This would not be easy for her—an abortion clinic worker surrounded all afternoon by people from Operation Rescue. "Wouldn't it be a great time to call the cops?" She smiled.

"I suppose so," I said. "They're all here!"

We walked in and were greeted with smiles, cheers, and hugs. About thirty-five people showed up for the baptism. An associate pastor from Hillcrest was there (Pastor Sheats was still on vacation), as was Carol Everett, a former abortion clinic owner. Peggy was the only reporter, except for the photographer from the *Dallas Morning News.*

To my surprise, many people brought presents. The director of the Garland Crisis Pregnancy Center gave me a slate ("Jesus erases all your sins," she explained); the woman from Hillcrest who had prayed with me to receive Jesus gave me a beautiful Belgium-lace cloth angel. It was the prettiest thing I had ever seen in my whole life. It was white, it was new, and it represented everything I felt as a new Christian. I almost wept when she told me she hoped it would go with my living room.

Ron Allen, another Hillcrest friend who had helped me with taxes, had a guitar and was playing some worship songs, and he finally called everybody outside for the actual baptism. It was

August in Dallas, so we weren't about to leave the air-conditioned house until we had to!

Flip called everybody together. He looked handsome, but out of character, in his tie. Flip's twin sons, David and Jason, came up to me and said, "Hey, Miss Norma, what do you think of Dad's clothes?"

"They look nice," I said.

"We had to dress him."

"Somebody has to."

"By the way," they added in a whisper. "The tie's ours."

"Figures," I said. (Later they would be very upset with their dad for wearing their tie in a pool filled with chlorine.)

As Flip began to speak, I found myself growing nervous. The reality of the symbolism was starting to take hold. Just as I had clung to Ronda when I went forward "to meet Jesus," so I clung to her now before my baptism. I was not going to leave her side.

Flip spoke briefly from Isaiah 61:

The Spirit of the Lord GOD is upon Me,
Because the LORD has anointed Me
To preach good tidings to the poor;
He has sent Me to heal the brokenhearted,
To proclaim liberty to the captives,
And the opening of the prison to those who are bound;

To proclaim the acceptable year of the LORD,
And the day of vengeance of our God;
To comfort all who mourn,
To console those who mourn in Zion,
To give them beauty for ashes,
The oil of joy for mourning,
The garment of praise for the spirit of heaviness;
That they may be called trees of righteousness,
The planting of the LORD, that He may be glorified.
(vv. 1–3)

Flip was wearing a microphone as he spoke, and after he finished he took my arm and tried to lead me into the water—still wearing the microphone.

"You're gonna meet the Lord a lot sooner than you think," I muttered, and Flip turned back toward me with a quizzical look on his face. I pointed toward the microphone, and he smiled. He took it off, handed it to someone else, and we waded into the pool.

It was an amazing thing for me to walk down into that water, turn around, and look at the people surrounding the pool. A few people were there from Hillcrest and from ABC (the camera crew), but other than that, they were mostly Operation Rescue folk. I had fought with each and every one of them corporately if not individually. Many of them had faced my anger, my cussing, my spitting. Yet every one of them was smiling.

Wow, I thought as I stood about waist-deep in the water, *I can't believe I'm actually doing this.* I wanted to do it, with all my heart. It's just that, two weeks before, all these people gathered poolside were the opposition. These people were the ones about whom Gloria had said, "We have to be careful." And now they were about to become my spiritual family.

The associate pastor from Hillcrest, Mike Ballard, prayed and read some more Scriptures. Then Flip said to me, "I'm going to put this rag on top of your face because you're going to go under the water."

I nodded.

"Norma McCorvey," Flip said out loud, "I baptize you in the name of the Father, the Son, and the Holy Spirit."

Flip placed the rag over my face, and I felt myself being lifted down. Just before I hit the water, Flip whispered, "Don't worry. I won't drop you."

Imagine this: the man I once called "Flip Venom, O.R. Terrorist," now had a rag over my face and was dunking my head underwater, all with my permission!

It was over so fast, I wanted to be dunked again. Though I knew my sins had already been forgiven in Jesus Christ, Flip had told me that the baptism symbolized all my sins being washed away. I felt clean, but I wanted to be dunked one more time, just for good measure. *After all,* I thought, *we've got a lot of sins to wash away here.*

But as soon as the sunshine hit my face, I realized that one dunk really was enough. Happiness exploded inside me. I grinned so widely that my face hurt—my muscles weren't used to what was a relatively rare expression for me. For many years I had forgotten how to smile, but now that old expression came racing back. The only time I had ever felt so light was the night I first asked Jesus into my heart.

Afterward there was a small reception. We had German chocolate cake with the words, "Norma, Alive in Christ, Eph. 2:3–7" printed in frosting. Carol Everett shared a few words, and one of the pastors present offered a closing prayer.

I could tell that Connie was still a little nervous. But for me, it was a highlight in my life, a new beginning for my life as Norma McCorvey, Christian.

I was baptized on Tuesday, August 8, 1995. Though ABC had covered it, the spot would not air for two days, and the photographer from the *Dallas Morning News* had agreed not to release the photos until after Peter Jennings ran the story on Thursday evening. It was a bold decision and a big concession on his part that later almost cost him his job—but he was determined to honor our wishes.

Since the world still did not know about what had happened, Ronda and I were able to have a little fun on Wednesday. Ross Perot was holding a big political meeting in Dallas, and Rescue was planning to be out in full force to plead the cause of the unborn. The international media were there by the planeload.

Ronda and I drove out to the airport to pick up some Rescue leaders who were flying in for an Operation Rescue leadership meeting. Ronda has night blindness and can't drive after dark, so I agreed to sit behind the wheel.

As we pulled onto the LBJ Highway and headed for the airport, both Ronda and I felt a little weird. In spite of all that had happened, the thought that both of us were driving together to the airport to pick up leaders for an Operation Rescue meeting still didn't seem right. We had been friends for a long time, but vocationally, we had always been bitter enemies.

But if it seemed funny to us, you should have seen the looks on the faces of the six Operation Rescue leaders we picked up at the airport! I'll always remember the look on Tom Raddell's face. Tom got off the plane, looked at me, dumbfounded, and said, "And your name would be Norma?"

"Yes."

"McCorvey?"

"Yes."

Tom knew who I was—he had seen my picture, read about my history, and even prayed for me. He just couldn't figure out why I was at the airport, picking him up. He knew Ronda and trusted her fully, but something just didn't seem right.

As inconspicuously as possible, Tom pulled one of the other leaders, named Sue, aside and began whispering in her ear. I knew exactly what he was saying: *What on earth is Norma McCorvey doing here?!*

Sue kept throwing furtive glances my way, trying not to stare yet fascinated by what she was seeing. I tried to break the ice by chatting. "You all must be tired flying in so late."

Yeah, they wanted to say, *but why do you care?*

I was new to all this. I had no idea what you were supposed to say to a bunch of rescuers arriving for a meeting. Christian and pro-life small talk were completely foreign concepts to me. These people were too polite to ask a potentially embarrassing question: "Why are *you* picking *us* up?!"

We all piled into Ronda's van, and I noticed a collective gasp when I climbed into the driver's seat. They realized that with one wrong turn I could wipe out a good number of O.R.'s leadership.

I finally winked at Ronda and said, "I don't think these friends understand what is going on."

Ronda laughed and said, "Did I introduce you all to Miss Norma?"

"I just can't believe that Norma McCorvey is picking us up," Tom said. "Does Flip know about this?"

I laughed out loud. This was fun. I could sense them thinking, *She's gonna wipe us all out! Does she really have to go fifty-five miles per hour in a sixty-mile-per-hour speed zone?*

Back at the hotel, Tom went to Flip and with tears in his eyes said, "Can you believe it? *Norma McCorvey!* I don't know how long I've prayed for her, but I can't believe she drove me to a Rescue meeting!"

I was touched to see how sincerely others had been moved. I thought I had made a deeply personal decision—and I had. But I was reminded just how public such decisions became when the former Jane Roe made them.

CHAPTER

25 Media Mayhem

Rule number one after becoming a Christian: wait a few years before you go on *Nightline*. I didn't follow that rule, and it proved to be a disaster.

In spite of my earlier misgivings about Peggy Wehmeyer, she did come through in the end. When she first mentioned the story to Peter Jennings, Peter reportedly said, "This represents a tremendous political shift in the abortion debate," but Peggy did her best to get him to see beyond the abortion issue.

"Peter," Peggy said, "look at the footage. Look at her kneeling on the playground, weeping. Watch her standing in a swimming pool being baptized. This is not a political shift—see it as it is!"

Peggy saw that the real story was about giving my heart to Christ, which was the reason for everything else that followed. The story ran on Thursday's edition of *World News Tonight with Peter Jennings* and was amazingly long. Many spots run fifteen to thirty seconds, but the story on my conversion ran for several minutes. After watching the spot, I felt a little bit better about having agreed to do the *Nightline* show later that evening.

Neither Flip nor Ronda thought I should do the *Nightline* interview. They were outspoken in asking me not to, but I felt confident enough to give it a go.

That was my first mistake.

"Can you go with me?" I asked Flip.

"I'm sorry, Miss Norma, I can't. You know we have a leadership meeting scheduled tonight. People have made plans to come here from all over the country."

So I went to the studio alone.

That was my second mistake.

I had met Ted Koppel in 1992 in Washington, D.C., and always thought it would be fun to be on his show. So when Ted's producer called me, I agreed to appear; but later, after Flip and the others questioned whether I should do it, I backed off and said I wasn't so sure.

Ted called me back personally and said, "I understand you're having second thoughts."

It was hard to explain why I did not want to do the program, especially after I had already accepted, so I gave a pretty lame excuse. "I don't really have any transportation," I said.

"What if I have a car pick you up and make sure you get downtown okay?"

Ted overcame each excuse I threw in front of him. Finally, I decided that since I had given my word, I should follow it up and do the show.

On Thursday evening, an assistant producer and a female reporter came to pick me up in a Lincoln Town Car. When we drove up in front of the ABC station in Dallas, hordes of reporters were waiting for us. The ABC story had just aired, there had been an announcement that I would be on *Nightline,* and a lot of international reporters were in town looking for something to do.

It was a madhouse around that studio.

"Duck, Norma, and they won't see you," the woman said.

I thought, *Why should I duck? I don't have anything to be afraid of.*

"Duck, Norma," the assistant producer said, more forcefully than his female counterpart, so I did.

I remember going through the gates, and the producer explained, "We're going to open the door. I want you to get out, run that direction, and go straight through the first door you see."

"Okay." At first I thought he was overreacting, until I looked behind me and saw a herd of reporters rushing toward our car, carrying cameras, and calling out my name. It was crazy.

I hurried inside and found the door led directly into the studio. An Asian woman looked at me and said, "What are you doing?"

"I'm going to be on *Nightline.*"

"Oh," she said, disgust in her tone, "I know who you are."

"Well, don't be biased or anything!" I said. She responded with a snort and a sneer.

I don't take any makeup, so they led me directly into the taping room, where a guy walked in and said, "You're *her*?" with a threatening look, then left without saying another word.

I couldn't believe it. Clearly, these people hated me. Since I had been a Christian for less than three weeks, my temper still had not been dealt with yet, and I could feel myself starting to boil.

Another guy walked into the room. He was smiling.

"Stop right there!" I challenged him. "If you've got anything mean to say, I don't want to hear it—"

"Norma," he broke in, "I'm a Christian."

Relief flooded me. *Finally, a friend.* "Come right in!" I said, a little too enthusiastically, I'm afraid.

He laughed. "You're not very well liked around here right now," he explained.

"So, what's new?" I said.

As I sat in the studio, a few people walked in. One was a proabortion reporter. "Need a little attention, is that it, Norma?" she sneered.

I snapped back at her. I had already had enough of this. If only she had known about the dozens of shows I had turned down.

"My, my, my, what a vicious web we weave," she taunted me. "How do you spell your pastor's name? Or do you even know his name?"

Now I was *very* angry. "It's Dr. Morris Sheats," I said. The abortion movement was trying to dismiss my conversion as a chance to get in the newspapers and on television. This was ridiculous.

An ABC technician came in and said, "I want you to turn around to the right. That would be this way."

He jerked his thumb in the right direction. So now they thought I was back in kindergarten?

I started fighting back. "You call yourself a professional?" I said. "I think not."

I'm a fighter by nature, and it doesn't take much to draw me into a scrap. These people had me just where they wanted me. I was absolutely furious by the time the interview started. I tried to remember all my professional training, but even then, I had to think to get the proabortion sound bites out of my head. When you've been representing legal abortion in interviews for so many years, it's hard to change gears.

Plus, when I get my temper up, it's extremely difficult for me to suddenly transform myself into a nice, pleasant personality. I am who I am. I've never been very good at putting on airs.

Calm down, Norma, I kept telling myself. *It's not worth it.* But I couldn't calm down. That blasted proabortion reporter wasn't about to let me.

Once the interview started, this same reporter, who of course was sitting off-camera, kept whispering something to me. I got confused and started looking at her, when Ted Koppel said, "You can look at me, Norma."

"Okay," I said, but I continued to be distracted by this woman in the studio. When I get flustered, I don't think too well.

So I was angry, confused, and about as new a Christian as you can be. My conversion was about Jesus more than anything else, but Ted kept asking me about abortion. I had not thought through that issue yet. The past three weeks had been consumed with new prayers, asking for people's forgiveness, and reading the Bible. All the ethical reflections were still very new, so in answer to one question, I even said, "I still support a woman's right to choose an abortion, in the first trimester only."

You see, my decision really *had* been about Jesus. I became a Christian to serve God, *not* to make a statement about abortion.

Instantly, I knew I had messed up. The woman's whispering, the hot lights, the anxiety of being on a national camera, all combined to make me feel nauseous. I just started to fall apart.

I tried to steer the conversation onto more fertile ground. When Ted asked me what had changed my views on abortion, I said cryptically, "It was because of what I saw in the freezer."

The most natural follow-up question for Ted would have been, "What was that?" but he opted for silence instead.

That was new to me. I was used to having reporters set me up. If I gave them the bait for a question they knew would have a provocative, pro-choice answer, they would be sure to take it. But now, everything had changed. I got clobbered, and I said some things that I later came to regret very much.

It was a difficult lesson. Thanks to Gloria, I had plenty of experience in front of a camera, but I soon discovered that I would have to learn everything all over again.

I did get to say a few important things. Ted let me explain that I felt I had been used by abortion-rights groups and that I was determined not to be used in the same way by pro-life groups. "There will not be any exploitation of my political status," I said. "I've already been exploited enough to last a lifetime."

I was touched when I learned that Gloria Allred backed me up on how I had been treated by the proabortion movement, agreeing that I had been treated poorly and then excluded from speaking events.

While I was on the air, the Operation Rescue leaders took time out from their conference to watch me on the screen. When they heard me say, "I still support a woman's right to choose an abortion in the first trimester only," there was a gasp and then a cringe on virtually every person's face.

Flip was not worried, and he tried to assure them. "She's a baby Christian," he told them. "Give her time."

I walked into the conference after the interview, and I sensed that something was wrong, but I couldn't put my finger on it. I walked farther into the lobby and saw Flip.

"Good show, Miss Norma," he said.

Yeah, right, I thought. I could sense some tension in his voice.

Several local television stations had followed me to the hotel for follow-up interviews. I pulled Flip aside and said, "I don't want to do any more press." It looked like we weren't going to have any choice, however.

"Come and sit with me, Miss Norma," Flip said.

My palms were shaky, and I could feel myself sweating. An inner tension was eating me up. I knew something had gone wrong, very wrong, but I just didn't know what it was.

Cameras kept coming up to me, but I felt myself shrinking inside. "Look at the camera and smile," Flip said.

I did. We were bombarded with sixty-second shots for the next half hour or so. Afterward, we went back upstairs to the O.R. meeting. I was afraid to face the leaders, but I wasn't sure why.

Pastor Bill Shanks, an O.R. leader from New Orleans, walked up to me and said, "Miss Norma, you're doing so good. I can see God in your eyes."

I was touched, overwhelmed, and flooded with relief. This was exactly what I needed to hear. When I was speaking for the proabortion movement, they took advantage of every opportunity to cut me down; so, instinctively, I thought it would be the same with the pro-lifers. Now that I had messed up and wasn't useful to them anymore, surely they would all disown me. That was my fear, anyway, and it was a frightening thought. The proaborts clearly hated me now. The media looked on me with disgust. If these people turned away from me . . .

"I want you to come down to New Orleans," Pastor Shanks added.

I was expecting to be disowned again, but he wanted me to visit him and speak again! I couldn't believe it! "I'll go if I can take Ronda with me," I said. I wasn't about to go anywhere alone for a while.

Later, as the urgent duties wound down, Flip took me aside again to see how I was doing. "They confused you, Miss Norma, didn't they?" he said. "They really got to you."

"Yeah," I said, then started crying. This was monumental. I *never* cried in public, but the whirlwind nature of the last two days just collapsed in on me.

"I don't want to see that," Flip said. "I can't bear to see you cry."

"I was scared to death," I said. "I wish you would have been there with me."

Both of us learned a lesson that day.

Now that the news was out, the floodgates of media mayhem were opened. Reporters began knocking on my door early the next morning. When I wouldn't answer, they started knocking on my windows, walking across my lawn, and calling out to me for "just one short interview." It was wild.

An NBC reporter was particularly persistent, and I thought, *Something has to give. If I do this one interview, everybody will understand, and they won't call me anymore. I won't be the exclusive story I am now.*

I could not have been more wrong. Again, the interview did not go well. I let the NBC reporter in and was completely caught by surprise when the interviewer started asking me about my "lesbian counterpart."

It took me a few seconds to realize what he meant. Connie and I had not slept together for years. Even so, Connie had been my lifelong friend. She had risked her life for me the night bullets tore into our house. She had driven me home from I don't know how many drunken sprees. We had been business partners, confidantes, you name it. And now, finally, we were entering a time in our lives when I could help Connie out. She was nearing retirement, and, finally, I might have a chance to repay her.

Yet this reporter, who didn't even know me or Connie or any of the intimate details of our lives, had the nerve to ask me, "Will you leave her now, Miss McCorvey?"

My first thought was, *It's none of your business!* I was angry and I let my emotions run ahead of my thoughts, and again, I said some things I didn't mean to say.

Not once that I can remember did any member of the media make an issue about my previously lesbian relationship with Connie. Not once. As long as I was supporting the proabortion movement, what I did behind closed doors was my business. But now that I was a Christian, every single reporter was fixated on my relationship with Connie. Suddenly the name Norma McCorvey rarely appeared by itself in print. Instead, it was "Norma McCorvey, formerly an admitted lesbian," or something similar.

Was this an accident? Was the former omission and current obsession merely coincidental? You tell me. There has been a great deal of speculation regarding the sexual orientation of several well-known women who support legalized abortion, but you don't see them questioned about it every time they get in front of a camera.

For the record, let me be perfectly clear: I now believe homosexuality is a sin. When Flip asked me, "Do you renounce the devil and his works, and the sinful desires of the flesh," he made it very clear to me that he would not baptize someone who intended to live the homosexual lifestyle, and I have never looked back.

But I was still figuring out just what the proper parameters were. Since it was obvious that the rules had changed dramatically, we began restricting our interviews to Christian media. Even so, the phones never stopped ringing for weeks. I'll never forget that sound. We couldn't answer them fast enough. As soon as one line was cleared, another line started screaming out that another call was coming through.

Emily did not understand all the attention I was receiving. She looked at Ronda and said, "How come the newspapers didn't call when I received Jesus into *my* heart?"

Pastor Sheats was still on vacation, but he made a special call to see how I was doing. I told him about the calls, and he said, "Norma, I think it's best if you don't do any interviews for now. They'll just confuse you." He urged me to begin reading the Gospel of John, and I was encouraged by his concern for me.

Even after repeated refusals for interviews, the phone would not stop ringing, so I finally put a message on my answering machine: "This is Norma McCorvey. There will be no press statements, there will be no more public appearances from me. I am going to be a regular person, Norma McCorvey."

Of course, that didn't stop the reporters from ringing my doorbell incessantly, knocking on the door or windows, and making a general nuisance of themselves. Let me tell you—when the media are on to a story, they do not know the meaning of the words *common courtesy.* They don't care what lawn they're stepping on, what bush they're trampling, what window they're peering through—until they get their story, quote, or photograph, they won't quit. If anybody else did what these people do, they would be arrested; but for some reason, as long as they're doing it as a member of the media, it's supposed to be okay.

Phil Donahue was one of those who called. He had approached me earlier, in 1989, through Gloria's office, and I had refused.

"Don't you want to be on *Donahue*?" Gloria had asked me.

"Not particularly," I said. "It's nothing personal. I just don't like his show. Now if Arsenio Hall calls, I'm listening."

Flip received the *Donahue* invitation and called me at home. At first, he tried to dissuade me from accepting, until I cut him off. "You don't have to convince me of anything, Flip. I don't want to do it."

I could almost hear Flip's relief. "Then can I have the pleasure of calling them back and being the one to tell them no?"

"Go right ahead."

I had expected some reaction from the U.S. media, but we received requests from Ireland, Canada, Australia, Denmark, and some places I'd be hard put to even find on a map. The international media have made this a very small world. The photograph taken of my baptism even made it to the front page of the *London Times*!

What amazed me was the difference between the attention given to my decision to accept Christ (and my corresponding conversion to pro-life), and the complete anonymity with which I had played the part of Jane Roe. I had to read the newspapers to find out about the *Roe v. Wade* verdict. Back then, nobody knew who I was, and, apparently, nobody cared—and that was just fine with me.

Now, all of a sudden, everybody wanted to talk to me, but I didn't want to talk to them. I was not trying to create news. I had no desire to be tomorrow's headline or to have my face appear above Dan Rather's shoulder on another nightly newscast. But the media kept coming.

There was another difference in the media's attitude toward me. Before, as Jane Roe, plaintiff in *Roe v. Wade,* I was somewhat of a media darling. Most of the national reporters are strongly proabortion, or at least what they call "moderately prochoice." Interviews were usually conducted on a friendly basis. Now I was "Norma McCorvey, Christian fundamentalist"—*the enemy.*

It took some time for me to adjust, and I got caught once or twice because of it.

Keep in mind, what you see on television is an *edited* version of what actually takes place. On an earlier occasion, long before I knew what Operation Rescue was all about, a television reporter asked me, "Miss McCorvey, what do you think about Operation Rescue?"

I had never heard of them. They had shown up outside our clinic one time, and mostly consisted of young couples carrying babies, pushing baby strollers, and generally behaving themselves. They were demonstrating, but I didn't pay that much attention. In fact, for some reason, I had thought they were pro-choice.

"Oh, I think they're great," I said.

The reporter stopped the interview, told the cameraman to stop rolling, then turned to me and said, "Oh no, Norma, they're the *opposition.*"

This woman was supposed to be reporting the news. On the air, it looked like she had been trying to get *my* opinion, but obviously, she was more interested in communicating *her* opinion. That type of thing got me angry, even if the person doing it was on my side.

"They're just doing their own thing," I argued. "Isn't that what America is all about?"

"But Norma, they want to *stop abortion.* How could you say anything good about them?"

The reporter would not let up. "Listen," I offered. "Do you want to bag the interview? We don't have to do this if you don't want to. If you want to find somebody else who will say mean things about this group, go right ahead."

After my conversion, this type of conversation, with the cameras turned off and the reporter discussing my answers, quickly became a thing of the past. Suddenly they were out to catch me, hoping I'd say something stupid or controversial.

Another reporter who really got to me was a woman from Austin who called and kept pressing for an interview in spite of my repeated refusals.

"Miss McCorvey," she said finally, "don't you think you owe us an explanation?" For the next thirty seconds, I did not act like a Christian. I let her have it up one way and down another.

What really bothered me was the suggestion that I had wronged her and the media and everyone else by choosing to accept Jesus Christ as my Lord and Savior and by admitting that abortion kills a life and should not be allowed.

I was not used to this uneasy relationship with the press, and I paid the price for my inexperience. If I confused any of you during this process, please forgive me. I am truly sorry.

Once the news of my baptism became public, I knew it was inevitable that I would get a call from Gloria. "A reporter just called me," Gloria explained, "and she wanted to know if I knew about what you had done."

"Well, what have I done?" I asked.

"She said you became a Christian."

"Well, Gloria, I kept after you for the better part of four years to make me an honorary Jewish person, but you wouldn't do it, so I just went and got some religion myself!"

My Book of Runes had never been enough. I was so thirsty for faith, and though I so greatly appreciated Gloria's faith in me—"Lean on me instead of leaning on the drugs and booze"—I knew that human companionship alone was not strong enough to break the destructive behaviors that ruled my life. I needed a supernatural power, and I needed a relationship with the God who created me.

Before I became a Christian, I understood intuitively that God was angry with me. I walked around, casting furtive glances up at the sky, wondering when God was going to get fed up and send down a lightning bolt with my name on it. That type of living makes you feel real old, real quick.

Gloria's friendship meant the world to me, and to this day I am grateful for what she did for me. But the love I have found in God is a love that means even more than the world means to me. It's a love I had to follow.

CHAPTER 26
One Hundred Percent Pro-Life

Because of my experience on *Nightline* and my deep desire for privacy, I decided not to read a newspaper or watch a single newscast until several weeks after my conversion, at which point I assumed my story would be old news.

Later, I learned how vehement some of the reactions were. Sarah Weddington got me furious (for the last time, since I'll never read another word of what she says) when she told a reporter that the only reason I converted was to get attention from the media. I was ducking interviews every chance I got. I wanted the press to leave me alone.

I've always wondered if Sarah didn't somehow resent me. Maybe she wanted the case to go down in history as *Weddington v. Wade*. Or maybe—this may be closer to the truth—she was resentful of the fact that I still had my child and hers would never return.

I don't know what it was, but she sure got into it with Flip on Bryant Gumbel's show. Flip let her have it when Sarah said, "Norma has every right to make this decision. *Roe* gave her that right."

As if I needed a Supreme Court case to give me the right to accept Jesus Christ as my Lord and Savior!

The truth came out in that interview. Sarah confessed, "I don't care about Norma McCorvey. I care about Jane Roe. Norma McCorvey was just a name on a class-action lawsuit."

This was exactly what I had felt. Ronda and Flip and Pastor Sheats and the folks at Hillcrest loved Norma McCorvey and were willing to overlook Jane Roe. The proaborts loved Jane Roe and despised Norma McCorvey. My Christian friends had learned to love a fallen person; my proabortion friends had despised the person and fallen in love with a myth—Jane Roe.

Opened Eyes

It wasn't until about a week after my appearance on *Nightline,* when I was working in O.R.'s office, that I had what I'd call my full pro-life conversion. I was answering phones, when all of a sudden I saw a poster on the floor.

I'm a neat freak—tidiness counts big time with me—so I picked up the poster and then immediately felt faint when I looked at it.

The poster depicted basic fetal development from conception through delivery. I started looking at the faces of the babies depicted on it, and the eyes of the children shook me.

The progression was so obvious, the eyes were so sweet. It hurt my heart, just looking at these unborn children. I've always heard that eyes are mirrors to the soul, and these mirrors were shockingly clear. I stared at the poster for a long time, studying it and reading all the captions, as if I were a medical student preparing for an exam.

Before I knew it, I was in tears again. I went outside real quick, fumbled for a cigarette, and just stood there.

Finally, it dawned on me.

Norma, I said to myself, *they're right.*

I had worked with pregnant women for years. I had been through three pregnancies and deliveries myself. I should have known. Yet something in that poster made me lose my breath. I kept seeing the picture of that tiny, ten-week-old embryo, and I said to myself, *That's a baby!* It's as if blinders fell off my eyes, and I suddenly understood the truth.

That's a baby!

I felt crushed. I felt so bad I just wanted to run, which is what I always did when I faced difficult truths before I became a Christian, but I knew that had to change. I had to face up to the awful reality. Abortion was not about "products of conception." It was not about "missed periods." It was about children being killed in their mothers' wombs.

All those years, I was wrong. Signing that affidavit, I was wrong. Working in an abortion clinic, I was wrong. No more of this first-trimester, second-trimester, third-trimester stuff. Abortion—at any point—was wrong. It was so clear. Painfully clear.

For many, many years, I always thought that the worst thing I had done was to place my children for adoption (though one was placed against my will). I didn't want them to be hurt. I thought I couldn't care for them, and I did what I thought was best at the time; but even so, I always thought of this as my greatest failure.

But in one moment, I realized that placing a child for adoption could be an act of great courage. The real despicable act, the real blight on my life, was being Jane Roe and helping to bring legalized abortion to this country. The very thing I was celebrated for on earth was the thing I would be most sorry for in heaven. The thing that brought me fame, notoriety, a movie deal, a couple of book contracts, media interviews galore—it was shameful. It was wrong. It was the worst thing I ever could have done.

The World Responds

"The poster child just jumped off the poster!" Bill Price, the head of Texans United for Life, commented.

After the shocking news of my baptism, editorials began filtering out examining my conversion. Again, I was surprised at the reaction. Dusty Nix of the *San Jose Mercury News*, very much a proabortion reporter, wrote that "this is a public-relations catastrophe of the first and worst order for abortion-rights folks." *Time* magazine apparently agreed, saying that "the pro-choice movement has taken a serious hit."

Andrew Sullivan wrote in the September 11, 1995, edition of the (proabortion) *New Republic:*

> The conversion of "Jane Roe" seems to me to be an event of far more importance than much of the media seem to think. The *New York Times,* emblematic of the elite media in general, provided so many caveats in its story that you might not have noticed the picture of the former abortion-rights campaigner being baptized in a suburban swimming pool. Of course, it was not a political conversion; it was a religious conversion and so, incomprehensible to many secular journalists and readers. . . .
>
> It is a given for many that rank-and-file members of the religious right are uniformly hard-nosed, uncaring zealots. In reality . . . many pro-lifers are human, sincere and genuine. They can seem, to the average person, far more empathetic than the rigid denizens of NARAL; and their quiet witness is slowly having an unanswered, unanswerable effect on their neighbors and fellow citizens. The conversion of Roe is a small symptom of the impact of this.

I was touched that an editor had finally gotten it right. After years of working in a cauldron of hatred, factional infighting, bitterness, and resentment, I was won by a people of love. Their love included telling me that I was a sinner, that abortion was an offense to God, and that I would someday pay for this activity if I did not repent. But it was a love that also showed me there was a way out, an opportunity to experience forgiveness, grace, and mercy.

I was won by love.

Another editorial that touched my heart was written by Flip Benham. In a newsletter announcing my conversion to O.R. supporters, Flip wrote:

> What impact has Miss Norma's conversion had in the ongoing battle between the two sides? According to most in the pro-abortion movement this change in Norma is simply a little blip on the radar screen. Sarah Weddington . . . said, "All Norma McCorvey did was sign an affidavit. She was a bit player in a class-action suit that gave all women the right to choose." . . .
>
> Sarah's comments are revealing. Weddington, Michelman, Yard, Ireland, *et al.* were always embarrassed of their drug-addicted, uneducated, alcoholic, lesbian, carnival barker from the wrong side of the tracks. The Vassar girls always had their snoots so high in the air, they never had time to look down and see the huddled masses or a precious young lady like Norma. Like their predecessor Margaret Sanger, they saw only a cause and never a person. People have never mattered to the enemy. It is only the cause that is important. . . .
>
> We see Norma's commitment to Christ differently. . . . Norma's conversion sheds light on the horrors of the abortion industry and the intolerance, duplicity, and manipulation in the politics of the "pro-choice" movement. Those who have been screaming intolerance the most have been found to be the most intolerant of all. . . .
>
> The "pro-choice" movement is more concerned about its cause and the mythical Jane Roe, but our God is concerned about the person of Norma McCorvey. This is what Norma found so attractive about Christianity. Somebody really cared about her, no matter how sordid her past. Jesus is truly the friend of sinners!

Having Fun

Waking up to the truth was not all so intense, however. For fun, we started going on our infamous "Midnight Runs." I signed up for a membership class at Hillcrest, which ran for thirteen weeks. To blow off steam, on the way home from class sometimes Ronda and I and her girls would stop off at the office—which, of course, happened to be right next door to the abortion clinic.

I knew that Arnie frequently spent the night at the office with his girlfriend. One night, I let slip that Arnie was the type of man who would scream if he saw his own shadow.

"Really?" Ronda and the girls asked.

"Really."

I started feeling a little mischievous, and I got the idea that it might be fun to turn on the vacuum cleaner and put it next to the vent.

"Miss Norma, what are you doing?" Emily asked.

"You'll see, sugar," I said and smiled.

When I put the vacuum cleaner up against the vent, making metal hit metal to get his attention, I started calling out, "Arrrnieee, Arrrnieee, you sleeping, Arnie? Dreaming about dead babies, Arnie?"

Ronda and the girls and I started laughing so hard that we had to sit down. Emily fell on the floor, holding her side while she giggled and laughed.

Sometimes, Emily would send Arnie a fax, writing in her cute little kid's script, "Please don't kill the babies."

The abortion battle and the spiritual warfare were so intense that we did this for fun more than anything else.

One evening, we pulled into the alley behind the clinic and our headlights caught Arnie and "Wanda" (not her real name) walking in the back. Arnie panicked, made his fingers look like a gun, and pointed at us. We couldn't help laughing. "He's gonna shoot us with his finger?" I yelled.

Then Arnie ran through the back door of the clinic and slammed it shut, leaving his girlfriend outside. She saw the shut door, yanked on it, discovered it was locked, then looked back at us. Arnie was not about to open that door. He was probably huddled somewhere inside. Wanda looked around and then started charging toward our van.

"She's crazy, Ronda, put this thing in reverse!" I called out.

Ronda jammed the van into reverse. I looked back at the building and saw Arnie open the door just a crack, peep out, and close it again, still leaving his girlfriend outside!

He really was a worm of a man. When Arnie's wife was stricken with breast cancer, he kept her in one room of the house as she lay dying, and at the other end of the house he kept his girlfriend.

Yet if he were the one dying, the abortion movement would hail him as a "visionary," a "man of integrity and courage," and a "hero for our time." In the minds of some, abortionists can do no wrong—provided they keep doing abortions.

Untangled

The next few weeks presented some interesting scenarios as I became untangled from the abortion movement. For starters, I still rode into work with Connie. She had the keys to the abortion clinic, and I had the keys to O.R. We would drive into the parking lot, Connie would open up the doors of the abortion clinic, and I'd open up the doors for O.R. and the crisis pregnancy center.

Even Ronda had problems with this scenario, but Flip allowed it, in part because I couldn't stand to wait in the abortion clinic until the O.R. people arrived. Connie usually got to the clinic around eight o'clock, and the first Rescue person didn't get in until nine.

At first, Connie let me stay inside the clinic and even answer the phones, but that didn't last long. "Abortion mill!" I'd answer. "No ma'am, sorry, we aren't killing any babies this week. Call back later."

Sometimes, when I was feeling particularly mischievous, I might say, "House of death. The ex-executioner speaking." Once I even told a woman, "I can't get you scheduled for an abortion, but I'd love to tell you about Jesus," and I gave her O.R.'s number to call back later in the day.

Connie finally caught on to what I was doing and wouldn't let me answer the phones anymore. I couldn't just sit in the abortion clinic and do nothing for an hour without feeling creepy, so I started waiting outside. That became too uncomfortable, so Flip finally gave me my own set of keys to O.R.'s offices.

I was finally a full-fledged, key-carrying member of Operation Rescue—100 percent Christian, 100 percent pro-life.

CHAPTER 27

First Steps

My initial pro-life protest left much to be desired. After my first fiasco, I thought they would never let me out of the computer room again.

It was a quiet day inside the office. The phones were not ringing very much, the mail had been answered and sorted, and I had completed the pile of data input from my "in" basket. Since I didn't have anything to do, I decided to take a walk outside and see what was going on.

Ronda, Rene, and Jessie Ann were sidewalk counseling. As women approached A Choice for Women, the trio tried to engage them in conversation and hand out some literature. Sometimes the client would stop. Other times, she wouldn't.

I can do this, I thought, only I put my own twist on it. With a few marching steps, I walked up to the glass door of A Choice for Women and started shaking it. It was locked, but I gave it a good rattle.

"Let me have those babies!" I yelled. "I'm an old woman, and I can't have my own!"

Wanda was inside the clinic, laughing, shaking her head like I had gone crazy. Connie—still employed at the clinic—came out, started laughing, and said, "Norma, have you lost your mind?"

I looked behind me, gave the door another good shake, and shouted out to the Rescue team, "Is this how you do it? Have I got it right? *Give me those babies!*"

Ronda looked horrified, as if I had dropped my clothes right on the spot. Rene and Jessie Ann were doubled over with laughter.

Ronda walked up to me and in a matter-of-fact voice said, "Miss Norma, this is *not* how we do it. We have a lot of teaching to do, and I suggest you go back inside the office."

I was not the only one who had a few lessons to learn, however. A few weeks later, Ronda was handing out material from Focus on the Family entitled "What Does God Say About Abortion?" To counteract this, A Choice for Women had managed to get a brochure of their own that purported to address the same thing, from a proabortion perspective.

One of the clinic workers, Lynn, saw Ronda counseling some of the clients, and waved her brochure in the window. She had a smug, teasing look on her face, as if to say, "Pass out as many as you want—we'll just refute it with these." Ronda could not believe that someone would use Scripture to justify abortion, and she shocked all of us—Lynn included—by shouting out, "You whore!"

Ronda never talked that way, and Lynn looked like she had seen Ronda's head swivel around on her shoulders.

"Excuse me?" I said loudly. Ronda looked as horrified as anyone else when she realized what she had just said.

"You need to get yourself into that office and kneel down before God and ask him for forgiveness!" I said. Then I grabbed her arm and led her into the Rescue offices. We marched into a counseling room, and I said, "Ronda, *pray*!"

Ronda didn't drop to her knees fast enough, so I gave her a little push. I waited for her to start speaking, but since she took a few seconds to compose her thoughts, I figured I had better start clearing it up with God real fast, before the lightning started to fall.

"Dear God," I said, "Ronda didn't mean what she said. We all say things we don't mean sometimes, and Ronda, I'm sure, is really sorry." I turned my head. "Aren't you, Ronda?"

Ronda nodded her head yes.

"See, God? She really didn't mean it. She's a good woman, and I hope you'll find it in your heart to forgive her."

It was a new sensation, finally being the one leading Ronda into repentance! But it showed me that Ronda was a real person. She, her daughter, and the rest of the people at Operation Rescue had won my heart by showing me God's love. Within a few short weeks, Lynn, also, would be won by love. Deep in her heart, Ronda knew it was love, not hate or name-calling, that would melt abortion workers' hearts. But in the heat of the battle, it's easy to forget and let something slip. None of us are perfect, I guess.

Invitations

"Miss Norma, would you like to come to our house for Thanksgiving?"

"Miss Norma, could we take you out for lunch after church?"

"Miss Norma, you're looking great today!"

As I lived my first few months as a Christian, I was overwhelmed with the love that flowed my way. The invitations were generous and frequent. Before, the only invitation I got was to the annual *Roe* remembrance dinner at a Unitarian church.

But now I had discovered a group of people for whom kindness and courtesy were not antiquated values, but the principles by which they lived their lives. At the abortion clinics, everybody covered their backsides; everybody wanted to lead. At the Rescue offices and at Hillcrest, I found people who were always going out of their way to serve others.

In late August someone sent me a picture of a billboard that announced, "Welcome to the Lord Jesus Christ, Norma!" It was one of the sweetest things I had ever heard of.

I even received letters from people I didn't know. One came from Alecia Klauk, an office manager for South Carolina Citizens for Life (the National Right to Life Committee affiliate in South Carolina).

> I just had to let you know how welcome you are as a member of the pro-life movement and one of God's people. Last night, my husband and I watched the ABC story with tears in our eyes, wondrously amazed with God's power to work and heal. . . .
>
> Based on your words, you struggle with guilt because of *Roe*. I want to tell you what I'm sure you have heard from Flip and countless others in the recent past: God loves you infinitely more than he hates your sin, evidenced by Christ. You are a precious creation of the Most High God, and he loves you more than you will ever know. . . .
>
> We as pro-lifers are certainly thrilled that you have seen the truth regarding abortion, but I am more excited about the condition of your soul.

A woman from Athens, Georgia, wrote to tell me that she had carried my picture in her Bible for years to remind her to pray for me. I received more positive mail in two weeks of being a pro-life Christian than I did in two decades of being abortion's poster child. It was overwhelming.

Sure, there were things I needed to learn—I wish I had a photograph of the Rescue people's faces when I talked about decorating the office for Halloween—and I would be lying if I did not admit to some rough moments and personal squabbles. But all in all, at the age of forty-eight, I embarked on a brand-new life.

Not all of it was entirely successful.

Girl Things

Shortly after I became a Christian, Ronda began teaching me how to do "girl things." She taught me how to wear camisoles and dresses and figure out all the womanly things that so many females take for granted. I could never understand what women meant when they said, "Well, that's winter black, I need a summer black dress." To me, black is black; I don't know how a color changes from season to season!

Ronda even encouraged me to try those dreaded panty hose. The only pair of nylons I had were at least twenty years old, but during one of my adventurous moods, I decided to wear them to an abortion protest. I learned that wearing old panty hose can be absolutely disastrous.

Let me explain.

Even after my conversion, the abortion mill continued to be a three-ring circus. The demonstrations and confrontations never let up. Mark Gabriel, one of Rescue's most persistent picketers, was at the back of the mill one afternoon, in part because the back of the mill was safer, legally speaking, than the front. (If you're in the back of the building, you're actually on city land, and therefore you're not trespassing and usually can't be arrested. If you hang around the front and the cops are in a bad mood, you can be picked up without any questions being asked.)

I was at the front of the clinic, within earshot of three women who were smoking cigarettes just outside the abortion mill. They heard Mark calling out from the back, "Arnie, repent! You're killing little babies, and we want you to stop right now!"

"Forget this," one of the clinic workers said. "I'm just gonna call the cops."

From personal experience I knew that clinic workers called the Dallas police on Mark so frequently that they had little patience with him. In fact, a year earlier, one call from the A to Z Clinic actually went like this:

"911."

"Hi, it's Kirsten Breedlove (a former abortion clinic worker)."

"Oh, hi, Kirsten. Is it Mark again?"

"Yep."

"We'll come get him."

So when I overheard the threat to call the cops, I ran into the Rescue offices, got my keys, and then went out to my truck. I pulled it around to the back of the clinic and called out, "Mark! Mark! The police are coming. You've got to get out of here!"

Mark started walking toward my truck, but he was too late. The squad cars had arrived. And now the circus became a three-ring show.

I got out of the truck and shouted, "Hurry, Mark, hurry!" but he kept taking his time.

The cops jumped out of their car and barked at me, "Stay right there." I froze, then heard something behind me and turned. To my horror, I felt my panty hose split.

Oh, no! I said to myself, then held my breath as I felt the nylons inching their way down toward my ankles. *How am I going to explain this?* I thought.

I started swaying and dancing, doing my best to keep my pantyhose up and salvage at least a piece of my dignity, when the cop took another look at me and said, "I thought I told you to stay still!"

"I'm trying!" I shot back. Since dancing had been ruled out, I did my best to be discreet as I reached around my waist, trying to pull up my pantyhose, which had now reached my knees, on the sly.

I pulled up my dress by mistake.

"What in the world are you doing?" the cop challenged me. "Are you okay?"

"No, I'm not," I said and started to walk toward him. "Since you've asked me—"

He got a horrified look on his face, put his hand up, and yelled, "You stay right there!"

"Okay. I can't really move, anyway."

The cop finally reached Mark, and Mark thought he could talk himself out of jail by showing the police officer photographs of aborted babies. The cop's partner was shaking his head in disgust, then looked up at me, watching me squirm.

"Ma'am, are you sure you're okay?" he asked.

"I'm having a crisis with my panty hose."

The police officer looked at me like I was nuts and said, "I've got *two* crazy people on my hands. What did I do to deserve this? Is that your truck?"

"Yes."

"I recommend you go back to the office."

"That's not a problem, sir." I wanted to get as far away as I could. I slipped inside my truck, drove around to the front, went into the bathroom, and tried to figure out where all the pieces of my panty hose had gone.

Is all this woman's stuff worth it? I asked myself.

I finally gave up—not on Jesus, but on panty hose.

"God," I said, "I'll pray to you and read my Bible every day, but please don't ever ask me to wear panty hose again."

CHAPTER

28 Exodus

Once I was out of the clinic and in Jesus' arms, Emily set her sights on the other workers. At first, I was shocked and even hurt—but Emily's a little evangelist and would not be stopped. When Ronda talked to her about not paying me as much attention as she used to, Emily said matter-of-factly, "But Norma already knows Jesus! Now I have to reach the others!"

As clients walked into A Choice for Women, Emily, Chelsey, and a friend would sit on a bench, right next to the abortion clinic door, and hold their baby dolls in their laps. Sometimes, Emily would even stand up and in a sweet, soft voice, say, "Please don't kill your baby. My mommy almost killed me, and I'm so glad she didn't."

Because of Emily's innocent demeanor, the clinic workers were powerless to do anything to stop her. Besides, she began to win their hearts as well.

Chelsey was also active, writing letters she would "send" next door. Two of the clinic workers wrote back:

> Hi Chelsey,
>
> Are you being a good girl? Write me a letter back, okay? Connie and Lynn say "hi" also. Bye.

Chelsey,

Hope you're having a good day! Tomorrow should be fun because we get to ride "the jeep"! Keep being sweet. Love you, Lynn.

P.S. Connie wants some ice cream.

One day, Lynn, the woman Ronda had called a whore, asked Emily what she hoped to get for her birthday.

"A jeep," Emily said. Ronda thought Emily meant a little plastic toy, so she gave her one. But the day after Emily's birthday, Lynn asked Emily again, "What didn't you get that you really wanted?"

"I wanted a real jeep," Emily said. To explain what she had hoped to get, she described the little battery-operated toy cars that are big enough for a child to sit in and "drive."

"I'll get you one," Lynn said.

"Yeah, right," Ronda answered, when Emily told her the news. Those jeeps cost over two hundred dollars.

I checked with Connie about this jeep—I didn't want the girls to be hurt. Connie assured me that Lynn really had bought a jeep, and several of the workers were putting it together in the clinic.

The next day, Emily was led outside and her eyes grew wide enough to cover the world when she saw that pink Barbie jeep sitting outside the doors of A Choice for Women. It was big enough for Emily and Chelsey to ride in together. It had a little phone, plastic windshield wipers, and moved along at the battery-powered clip of about two miles an hour. Lynn and Sam and Connie had a great time showing Emily how everything worked. I created a couple of fake driver's licenses and presented them to Emily and Chelsey.

We ended up calling that jeep the "lifemobile." Emily never forgot why she was at the clinic. She started driving her jeep up to meet clients—it was so cute, the clients simply had to stop and talk to her. And Emily took advantage of the opportunity to give them some pro-life literature and ask them not to kill their babies.

Who knows how many lives this little girl has saved?

Evicted

God's timing is so precise it makes a Swiss watch look like something out of a Cracker Jack box. About three weeks after I was baptized, the landlord filed a petition for eviction against Operation Rescue. He denied that he had ever told O.R. they could stay rent-free until the abortion clinic moved out, though a clause in the lease did state that while O.R. was in the building, any other lease "to any medical or other group will specifically prohibit the advocating, encouraging, or performing of abortions."

There is no way the landlord could have approved that lease had he not originally intended to kick the abortion clinic out. And the rent-free agreement had been cited in numerous newspaper articles just after O.R. moved in.

The eviction petition came before a jury, which ruled a week later that O.R. did not have to pay back rent but did have to leave. Operation Rescue was allowed to remain on the premises until April 15, 1996.

Altogether, they were there for a year and two weeks.

When O.R. moved out, Flip laughed and said, "We just stopped in long enough to pick up Miss Norma."

I shudder to think what would have happened had Rescue not moved next door. There was just a small window of time when I worked at A Choice for Women and when Rescue needed to relocate. God's timing is amazing.

Over the next several months six other people followed me out of the abortion clinic. Three of them, including Connie and Kirsten Breedlove (Mark's former nemesis), became Christians.

The exodus became so pervasive that Arnie made every employee sign this contract:

A Choice for Women, PA
Gynecological Healthcare
Confidential Memo

> Please note that any contact between staff employees of A CHOICE FOR WOMEN and member (*sic*) of OPERATION RESCUE will not be tolerated during office hours. Contact after hours is considered immorale (*sic*). In either case any such contact may result in termination of the employment.

Arnie had feared an attack from Operation Rescue, not a voluntary exodus within A Choice for Women. His entire staff, except for Wanda, his girlfriend, eventually left. The memo was not effective. Workers saw the love of the Christians, recognized it for what it was, and began leaving in droves.

It's as if God decided to lift our blinders at the same time, as several of us realized we could not stay in the business of killing children any longer. For Connie, it happened when she was assisting in an abortion and, as she puts it, "a baby fell into my hands. I had thought it was just a muscle until then. I almost lost it. It tore my insides out."

Clearly, this exodus was not just about me. This was a movement of God, as he sovereignly decided to show tremendous mercy to a group of bitter, cynical, and hurting women trapped inside the abortion industry. We were delivered, and we have never been the same since.

Flip likes to explain it this way: "Theology is becoming biography." The gospel message is taking hold in the lives of women whom you'd least expect to give their hearts to Jesus Christ.

Not surprisingly, one of the biggest changes for me came with how I relate to children.

Children

"Well, hello there, sugar. What's your name, darling?"

The little one-year-old girl looked down at her feet. I lifted Rebekah into my arms and smiled at her cute little face. She smiled back.

Smiles such as these have been some of the biggest blessings about my conversion to Jesus Christ. For so many years I intentionally avoided little children. I knew what we were doing in the clinic from Thursday through Saturday, so the thought of getting attached to a child was just too threatening emotionally.

But since Emily pushed through, practically *insisting* that we become friends and providing me with a daily dose of the best kid hugs I've ever had, it is almost impossible for me to pass by little children and not at least acknowledge their presence and send a smile their way.

Ironically enough, it's a part of who I am. I just love children.

I count this as a miracle. I've seen people grow harder as they grow older, and I think, except for Christ, that would have been true of me. My issues with children were so blatant, I might have become that scary woman at the end of the street whose house the children are afraid to pass by.

I carefully set Rebekah back down. "She's adorable," I told her mother, who gave me a warm smile in return.

"Thank you," she said.

It dawned on me that I've never had a woman get up to leave an abortion clinic, smile at me, and say, "Thank you" before she walked out the door.

Learning Love's Lessons

A few weeks after Connie became a Christian, she joined me for our first mutual pro-life protest, a Life Chain. Connie and I had been to many, many demonstrations together, but we had always been on the other side. Ron Mackey was in charge of the particular "link" in which we stood—each church was assigned a certain portion of the street, and Ron was heading up Hillcrest's contingent. At a Life Chain, people peacefully stand a few feet apart on a public sidewalk, holding signs that say, "Abortion Kills Children" and a few "Jesus Forgives and Heals."

Connie and I had barely gotten our signs up in the air when a souped-up car drove past, and a guy leaned out the window, shouting something too crude to repeat here.

"You're nothing but a bunch of barnyard animals!" Connie yelled back.

Ron was horrified. "Miss Connie," he said, "we're not allowed to yell back at them."

Connie looked at Ron like he was crazy. "You mean we can't say *anything?*"

"That's right. Nothing."

"Even if they yell at us first?"

"Even if they yell at us first. If you're holding a sign, you have to just take it and pray for them."

Connie caught my eye with a look of protest, dropped her sign to her side, and took three steps back. "Do you mean to tell me," she asked Ron, "that not only am I not allowed to yell back at them, but I'm supposed to pray for them?"

"That's right," Ron said. "That's how we do it."

"Oh, man, nobody told me about that rule," she said.

She wasn't so sure she liked this particular pro-life tactic—but we had to remind each other: love was what won *us,* and love was what would win others.

Not long after that, I got an uncharacteristic craving for pizza. Due to my lactose intolerance, I'm not supposed to eat pizza, but it was near midnight and one of those situations where the hunger keeps attacking you in waves. You try to ignore it, but fifteen minutes later it comes back, stronger than ever—and when you're that hungry, nothing sounds as filling as pizza, lactose intolerance or not.

And then, as if to tease me beyond the point of human endurance, Domino's Pizza ran a tempting commercial. The pizza was steaming, the cheese looked tantalizing, and the tomato sauce looked so good I could almost taste it. As many people know, the owner of Domino's Pizza is a generous Christian man who gives money to many conservative causes, including pro-life organizations. The proabortion movement has been boycotting him for years.

I watched that commercial for thirty delectable seconds, then turned around and said to Connie, "Gee, I wish we could have Domino's pizza. It looks *so* good."

"We can, Norma," Connie said. "Remember? We're pro-life now."

"That's right!" I exclaimed. "What are we waiting for?"

Everything seemed to be grand. Little did I know that I was about to face the most difficult test I could imagine. Within days, I would lose one of the people I loved most in this world.

CHAPTER 29

Daddy

Even this once archfeminist has to admit that there's something inside a girl that will not allow her to outgrow the need for her daddy.

One night when I was still very young, about seven or eight, I heard my parents begin to tear into each other. They had fought many times before, but the intensity of this particular fight set it off as something distinct. There was a despair in my mother's tone, a sharp antagonism in my father's, and from upstairs it sounded as if violence could erupt any second. I remember huddling under my blankets in the night, waiting for the fight to come to an end, wondering if it would work its way upstairs.

The next day I skipped home from school and rushed into the house. Something was missing. I sniffed real hard, searching for the sweet smell of my father's tobacco, but it was nowhere to be found.

I asked my brother, "Where's Daddy?"

"He's not here."

He's not here. Those are frightful words for a young girl. I knew they meant much more than a temporary absence too. A young girl just knows these things. He was gone.

My father did not come back the next day, or the next day, or the day after that. My mother never sat us kids down and explained what had happened. She never actually told us that our father would not be coming back. She just assumed that we would figure it out eventually.

Then, a few weeks later, I came home from school and saw my father's shirt lying in front of the door. Happiness exploded inside of me. *That's Dad's shirt!* I thought. *He must be home!*

All of a sudden, I realized how much I missed him. Now that he was home, I desperately wanted a hug. I ran through the house shouting, "Dad, Dad, it's me! I'm home!"

The excited pitch of my voice carried through the first few rooms, but the responding silence was so thick and heavy that by the time I made it to the last room, my voice was nothing but a muffled whisper.

"I'm home," I finally sighed, "but I guess you're not."

Mom was just using his clothes for us to wipe our feet on.

It was a cruel act, by any standard, and one in which I refused to participate. I resolved to track dirt all over the house before I would rub my muddy shoes on Daddy's clothes.

Two years later, I was snug in bed when I noticed my door being opened. In a moment I felt my body being lifted, blankets and all, as my father carried me out to the station wagon. "We're moving, sweetie," he whispered. It felt so good to be back in his arms that I just lay there and smiled. He seemed so strong.

"I'm never gonna have to leave you again, Norma," he said. "We'll always be together from here on out."

And we were.

Men and Norma McCorvey never got along very well. They would use me for pleasure, get me pregnant, beat me up a bit, and then, invariably, leave. My father was the only real male figure who cared; he's the only one who stayed by me.

The Near Abortion of Jane Roe

I'll never forget the night I went into my father's room to tell him I was pregnant with the *Roe* baby. I had already made up my mind that I was going to have an abortion, but Daddy had a story he wanted to tell me first. In yet another irony in this crazy life of mine, I learned that Norma McCorvey, Jane Roe of *Roe v. Wade,* was almost aborted herself.

A few months after I had been conceived, my father went to town to pick up some things at the old country store in Lettesworth, Louisiana. Lettesworth is a very small community with far more pine trees than people and plenty of swamps between its forested borders and the sixty-mile stretch south to Baton Rouge.

The owner of the store looked up, saw my dad, and asked him, "Well, now, did your wife kill your baby?"

Dad said, "I don't know what you're talking about."

"Well, you know Miss Mary (referring to my mom) went to see Miss Mary Lee down the lane."

Miss Mary Lee was the woman who aborted all the babies in Lettesworth. For this she had earned a nefarious reputation, and respectable women of childbearing age would not be caught going down that lane unless they had strong intentions. Certainly, my mother wouldn't have gone there on a social call.

"You must be thinking about somebody else," Dad protested, "because my wife wouldn't do that. She's got a husband, that's me, so she don't need no abortion."

Dad confronted Mom later that evening. "Did you go see Miss Mary Lee?"

Mom sighed. Lettesworth was too small a town to keep secrets like this from your husband. "Yes," she said.

"What for?"

"It don't matter," she answered. "Miss Mary Lee said I'm too far along. She can't do anything to the child without possibly hurting me."

"Does that mean," I asked my dad, "that if Mom had found out about me sooner, I wouldn't be here?"

Dad nodded. He didn't want me to get an abortion. He stroked my hair and said, "You know, Norm, it don't make no difference how you got that way. We can take care of that baby."

We had a crazy relationship, we really did. When we lived together for a while, he tried to pick up my girlfriends, and I tried to pick up his. I could get drunk and call him at any hour of the day—midnight, 2 A.M., 4 A.M., it didn't matter—and he'd come and get me. There was never a lecture, never a scolding. He had left me once, and now that he had come back, he had promised he'd always be there and he was.

Sometimes, when I acted up, I thought it would have been easier on me if he had hit me, or at least verbally abused me, but he never did. He just picked me up, put me in the car, and took me home. The next morning he never mentioned the episode, even though he knew I'd probably end up calling him late at night in another few days.

"Too Mean to Die"

Shortly after Christmas 1995 I got a call from my mother. "Norma, you need to visit your father," she said. "He's dying."

I called the home where Dad was staying and talked to a nurse. "Is he dying?" I asked outright. I'm the type of person who wants to know the complete story right away.

"Honey, we all dying," the nurse said, "but he's not dying today, if that's what you mean. He's too mean to die."

I laughed. That sounded like Daddy. Still, I wanted to visit him, just in case.

As I walked up to my father's bedside I saw a man so weak he hardly resembled the strong figure who had once gathered me up into his arms late at night, and who, later in life, had supported my drunken body as I stumbled into bed.

"Daddy," I explained, "I've come back to God. I'm not afraid to go to church anymore. It's okay for me to do this now, Daddy. I just know it."

He smiled.

I handed him a pro-life T-shirt that read, "Pro-life without compromise, without exception, without excuse. Jesus is the standard." He looked it over, and though he was too weak to talk, he gave me a big thumbs-up sign. That was his way of telling me he supported what I was doing. Few things have meant more to me in my entire life than seeing my precious father stick his thumb in the air and smile.

A few days later, I was working at the Rescue offices when I got a phone call. "Norma McCorvey, please."

"Speaking."

"Is your father Olin J. Nelson?"

"Yes."

"Your father expired at 12:25."

"What?"

"Your father died just after noon."

The next few hours are a blur. I dropped the phone and started bawling. "It's not true, it's not true," I screamed. "Someone's playing a prank joke, and they're so cruel."

Ronda rushed up to my desk. "What is it, Miss Norma? What did they say?"

Crank calls are not exactly rare at the Rescue office, but she had never seen me get bent out of shape by one.

"They said my father has died, but I know he's alive. I know he is. I'm gonna go see him right now."

Ronda took over. "Just a minute, Norma," she said. "Let me handle this."

She called the nursing home. It was 12:45. "That's right," they confirmed. "He died about twenty minutes ago."

Ronda broke the news to me as gently as she could: my father was gone. "Norma," she said. "It's true. I'm really sorry, but it's true."

I still couldn't believe it. "It's *not* true, it's not true," I kept saying. "I'm gonna go see him. Right now. I'm gonna go see him."

Connie came to pick me up, but I still had not accepted the fact that my father had died. He said he would always be there for me, and I believed him.

Somehow, I got through that horrible day. Ronda and Flip got me to open up and talk, and by the end of the next day, I was finally able to pray, "Lord, I don't know if my dad's gonna be up there or not, but I sure hope so. I want to know that you'll take care of him. He was always complaining about how tired he was. Please let him get some rest now."

Losing my father was one of the most devastating experiences of my life. If I had not become a Christian six months earlier, I'm sure I would have attempted to take my own life in a vain attempt to join him. God did not arrive in my heart any too soon, believe me.

Now, after praying and saying good-bye, I felt like I could go on, confident that the Lord was going to take care of my dad.

One Last Cup of Coffee

Three women in New York had spent the better part of three years making a documentary of my life, to be aired on a cable television station. They had interviewed my dad earlier in the year, and I received a packet in the mail with their return address. Puzzled, I opened up the package and found a videotape of their interview with my father.

My hands shook as I realized these women had given me a chance to live a few more moments with my father. I got out some French Roast coffee—my dad and I are big coffee drinkers—and sat down for a final "coffee-drinking chat" with my dad.

I laughed and cried as I watched and listened to the man to whom I owed my life. His jet-black hair, his small frame, his supple smile, his ability to tell a story (only about 10 percent of which would be true)—all made me laugh, made me cry, and tore me up inside. But with the Lord in my heart, it was a gentle tearing. There wasn't despair, only sorrow.

I realized again how much Jesus meant to me. Just after I became a Christian, Jesus helped me come to terms with what I had done as Jane Roe. I could not "unsign" the affidavit. My change of mind had no impact on the law. But Jesus had brought me through repentance and feelings of tremendous shame until I could receive his mercy and forgiveness.

Now I was learning that the presence of Jesus was sufficient not just to help me come to grips with my past, but also to walk into the future—even a future without my dad. I'd like to share with you the words I spoke at my dad's funeral. It will help you understand how important it was to me that I could face my father's death within the experience of faith in Jesus Christ.

Passing of a Parent/Friend
Norma Leah McCorvey
January 4, 1996

My father, Olin J. Nelson, passed away at 12:25 P.M. on December 28, 1995. I stand before you to honor him and his life here on earth. My father was seventy-eight years old.

My father and I were very close, closer than most fathers and daughters. We were the best of friends. I could go to him with anything and never be afraid of what he would do or say.

I remember coming home from the doctor's office after learning I was pregnant for the third time. I told my dad. He stared at me for a few seconds and then smiled and said he was glad for me. He asked if I knew who the father was. He was willing to get a second job to help support the baby and me. I told him, "No, Daddy, I don't want to keep it."

I wanted an abortion, but I couldn't do it. God would not let me. Dad told me that my mother had considered aborting her second baby. That second child was me. He heard about that piece of history in the town's only store.

I tell you this because I want all of you to have a sense of what my father taught me. He grew with me, not outgrowing me. He waited for me to have a better sense of judgment.

On December 23, Pastor Sheats spoke to us about letting things go: bitterness, guilt, fear, doubt. He asked us to come to the altar to be healed of whatever was making us miserable. I went to the altar that Saturday evening and knelt on the floor with many of you. Jesus met us there, and I released the hatred I had for my mother. I asked for this in the name of the Father, Jesus, and the Holy Spirit.

On December 30, in his Sunday sermon, Pastor Sheats said that we all should have closure for the year 1995. The past belongs in Father God's hands. There is nothing we can do but trust him.

In this beautiful chapel, on this glorious day, with the time and season God gives to heal, you can all help me to make closure in saying good-bye to my earthly father.

Every time I see a flower bloom or a robin fly, I will think of my dad and smile. I love you, Daddy.

Good-bye.

CHAPTER 30
Empty Playgrounds

Four days after my conversion in July 1995, I went back to church with Ronda and her family. We got there a few minutes early, so I took Chelsey out to the playground. As I watched her play—Chelsey was the only child out there—I thought to myself, *This place looks so sad.*

A few minutes later we went inside, where Ronda directed me to a Wednesday night educational class. But something inside me would not let me stay. I felt very restless, so I got up and walked back outside. I felt drawn to the playground. Something—or Someone—was leading me there.

The playground was completely empty now. I sat down on a bench and studied the scene. *Why does this make me so sad?* I wondered. And then I remembered another empty playground.

One morning in the 1980s, when I was first letting the world know that I was Jane Roe, I was driving down Schroeder Road in Dallas, Texas. I looked off to my right and saw a school with an empty playground. Though I had probably passed this school more times than I could count, that day it seemed particularly significant for some reason. It was such a sad, sad sight and the still swings, the vacant slides, and the untouched monkey bars threw their emptiness into my soul.

But why? I thought. There is no fighting or arguing or crying on this empty playground. No earsplitting shrieks. No one is running out into the street. You don't hear or see any of those pesky things that happen when kids are around, not on this empty playground. It was a quiet world, the world we in the abortion movement were fighting for.

In fact, an empty playground meant less taxes. It meant there would be no childcare to pay, so women and men could pursue their careers with abandon. It meant that couples could live together and break up without the worry of who gets saddled with custody. *That's what an empty playground means,* I tried to tell myself.

But another voice was speaking, this one deep inside of me. I realized that in an empty playground there might not be any fighting or spitting or crying, but there was also no laughter, no smiles, no giggling, no pretty little curls bobbing on top of a five year old's head. There were no songs, no games, no shouts of triumph. There was just nothing, and nothing suddenly seemed terribly frightening.

The sight of that empty playground blew me away. I jammed on the brakes and pulled over to the curb. Something spiritual was happening to me.

Pull yourself together, Norma, I said to myself. *It's mid summer. School is out. There's no reason for the playground to be full.*

But I took one long look at that empty playground and that other voice deep inside me said, *It's all your fault, Norma. You're the reason this playground—and playgrounds all across this country—are empty.*

The swing started swaying slowly through a slight breeze, as if an invisible child had somehow climbed up onto the black rubber seat and started moving. I couldn't take my eyes off the playground, and I couldn't move my car. I wanted to will it full of children, but I couldn't. To this day, I can't honestly tell you how long I was there. I don't have any idea.

Finally, I felt that old familiar burning behind my eyes as the first few tears worked their way to the surface. How many times on how many interviews had I warned about the "problem" of raising children? With how much fervor had I mentioned all the trials a child can bring to a mother's life? We talked about unborn children as a threat to a mother's health, a drain on her pocketbook, a reminder of a disastrous relationship or rape; but we never mentioned the wonderful sound of a giggle. We never talked about sun dropping onto a little girl's golden hair. We didn't speak of a little boy's intense concentration as he tried to hit his first baseball. We never mentioned the music of a group of children playing ring-around-a-rosy.

I felt so sad. *What would this world be like,* I thought, *if there weren't any children? If the only people left were grown-ups, with our adult problems and our adult decisions and our adult self-interest? What kind of world would that be?*

I couldn't think about it any longer. It was too painful. I forced myself to turn on the ignition, put my car in drive, and took off, the empty swing still swaying gently with the wind.

Here I was, years later, mesmerized by another empty playground. In spite of my new beginning in Christ, the emotional pain was suddenly more than I could bear. Sobs erupted within me. The tears I shed were not gentle ones. They were coarse, they were hard, and they literally hurt as they forced their way out of my eyes. I thought I was losing it, but in reality, God was washing my soul in repentance for my role in *Roe v. Wade*. I did not fully understand it at the time, but this was a cleansing cry, not a despairing one.

I saw some people entering the church and waved one of them over. Speaking through my sobs, I told the woman, "Please get Ronda."

The woman thought I said "Wanda" and spent the next twenty minutes going through the rooms at Hillcrest, asking if anybody knew a Wanda. Nobody did. One of the people she approached was Ronda.

"Do you know a Wanda?" she asked.

"Here?" Ronda said. "No."

"Well, there's a woman outside, and she's upset—"

"I'm sorry," Ronda cut in, "but I don't know any Wanda, and I brought a friend with me tonight, a brand-new Christian, whom I can't find. I really can't stop to talk."

As the search for Ronda was going on, I calmed myself enough to start writing down some of my thoughts. Phil Keaggy has since put some of this to music:

Dear Lord, I sit across from a playground
that I visited this eve with a small child.
I know of such places where children play
and I know I'm the cause of them not being
filled with laughter and joy.
These grounds are empty
because the innocent children were killed—
dead because of the sins that I committed.

I hope, Lord, that there is a wondrous playground
that you have in heaven,
one that is well-guarded with angels
who will protect these children
and keep them safe and happy.

Lord, please make them smile and laugh up there
so that, when the glorious day comes
when I'm brought up to heaven,
the children will not hold this sin against me. Every time I see
an empty playground, I pray
with all my heart that yours will be full.

The sun is setting low, now,
and my heart hurts for the children

who have been torn apart by abortion.
I hope that you can put them back together
and make them whole.
If you like, Lord, you can use my body parts
in order to make these children whole—
I'll give myself up gladly.

I know, Lord, that you can do this,
if not only for them,
for the love that I have for each and all.
For God, you gave your only Son
and his shed blood for us.
You offered your body so that we could be whole.

Yet all I did was give my baby away
so that other women could tear theirs apart.
For that, I'll never be able
to look you in the face without shame.

Ronda finally made her way outside. When she saw me, she rushed over to the bench where I was sitting. A new wave of tears had swept over me—more a wail than a weeping. "Miss Norma," she said, "are you okay?"

"I wrote a poem," I said, sobbing, trying to find a way to express the deep anguish I felt inside.

"That's nice," Ronda said. It was dark out, she could barely read the words, and she was more concerned with why I was weeping so profusely than with anything I had written.

"That's why I'm crying," I said.

Ronda hugged me—a long, hard hug, the kind that breathes new life into the hurting. After a few more minutes, I was finally able to leave the playground under my own strength.

Ronda took the poem with her, and it was not until later that night that she actually read it. Her heart sank as she finally understood the depth of my sorrow. She immediately faxed the poem over to Flip.

The next day, Flip mentioned that he saw my poem. Then he put his arm around me and gave me a hug. "Miss Norma," he said, "I want to show you something. I have some good news for you."

Flip took that big black Bible of his and flipped it open to the Psalms. He began to read out loud: "I sought the LORD, and He heard me, / And delivered me from all my fears. / They looked to Him and were radiant, / And their faces were not ashamed" (34:4–5).

It was so hard for me to conceive that the Lord had forgiven me—especially after so many children had been killed. But he has forgiven me and restored me. And, gradually, I have learned to trust his Word more than my own feelings. Now I can sincerely say, "I look to him and I am radiant, and my face is not ashamed."

Some of the women and men reading this account may, like me, have become Christians, but are still struggling with the same guilt I felt over my role in previous abortions. I want you to know something. God has forgiven me for allowing my name to go on that affidavit. He has forgiven me for writing a book celebrating my advocacy of abortion. He has forgiven me for going on radio and television and talking to reporters, arguing to keep abortion legal. And he has forgiven me for actually participating in hundreds of abortions over the years.

Not one Christian I have talked to—not Pastor Morris Sheats, not Ronda Mackey, not Randy Terry, not Flip Benham, or any of the thousands of Christians who have since heard my testimony—has ever doubted that God has forgiven me. The only person who had trouble believing that I was really forgiven was me.

Even today I keep reminding myself of that Scripture, "If anyone is in Christ, he is a new creation; old things have passed away; behold, all things have become new" (2 Cor. 5:17). Another helpful verse is 1 John 1:9, which says that "if we confess our sins, He is faithful and just to forgive us our sins and to cleanse us from all unrighteousness."

If God can forgive Norma McCorvey—*Jane Roe*—and her role in abortion, surely he can forgive you as well. Like me, you will need to repent of what you have done, but you will receive the same peace and forgiveness that I now enjoy.

Please don't hold on to that guilt. Talk to your pastor. Go through a Bible study on postabortion syndrome. (Contact your local crisis pregnancy center, or write CareNet at 109 Carpenter Drive, Suite 100, Sterling, VA 20164.)

You can't undo your abortion any more than I can undo all the things I've done to make and keep abortion legal—but we can be forgiven. We can also work to present the cause of life in the future. But to do that, we need to be healed, and healing always starts with forgiveness.

I can't make my past go away. It's already written in the history books. On Judgment Day, there will be a multitude of witnesses to the wrongs I've done. Women will be able to point at me and say, "She was right beside me when I got my abortion, and she did nothing to stop it."

But my hope is the same as yours. I will not stand at the judgment seat of Christ alone, and neither will you. "We have an Advocate"—one who speaks to the Father in our defense—"Jesus Christ the righteous" (1 John 2:1).

Although I cannot make my past go away, I can do some things that help make amends. That is how I spend my time these days, working to preserve life, not destroy it. And my pro-life activities have taken me all the way to the Supreme Court.

CHAPTER 31

Making Amends

In April 1996 I returned to the Supreme Court where, in 1972, Sarah Weddington had argued on my behalf that women should be able to obtain a legal abortion.

A soft, steady rain was falling as I approached the marble steps of the Supreme Court. A video of my conversion, *Reversing Roe: The Norma McCorvey Story*, had just been released, and I was there to take complementary copies to members of the United States Supreme Court.

I couldn't unsign the affidavit the justices had already argued and decided upon, but perhaps I could, through the video, help them see the lies behind that fateful decision. And then, perhaps, they would decide to hear a case in which *Roe v. Wade* might be overturned. Nothing would please me more than to have *Roe* wiped off the books.

After delivering the videos to a courier, I went back outside. A steady drizzle continued to fall. My business was not done, however. I had something even more important to do. Before I became a Christian, I thought political action was the most important thing. Now I realized there was a much more powerful activity available to those who desire change: prayer.

At a news conference earlier in the day, I had explained my visit to the Supreme Court and the purpose of the *Reversing Roe* video. Now I wished the reporters would just go away. What I had to do next was not about getting my name in the newspapers or my picture on television—it was about fulfilling a personal mission.

I started to kneel down on the steps, when a police officer came up and said such an action would not be allowed. Not to be defeated, I walked down the steps to the sidewalk, and there I knelt in the rain, praying that what I had done might be overturned.

My prayer went something like this: "Lord, please let these justices come to know the truth about abortion. Let them understand in their hearts that it's wrong, and that they need to reconsider their decision."

Rain fell on my back and head as I knelt there. It seemed as if heaven itself were crying. My own tears fell on an already wet sidewalk.

"Please, God" I pleaded, "please, open their eyes as you opened mine. Help them to see the truth."

One of the "truths" I wanted people to see involved an admission I had made many years before. As Sarah Weddington presented my case, she used the fact that I had claimed to have become pregnant through a gang rape. The public had certain misgivings about abortion in the early seventies, but there was much greater acceptance of abortion in cases of rape, so even though I wasn't really raped, I thought saying so would garner greater public support.

This means that the abortion case that destroyed every state law protecting the unborn was based on a lie.

Pushed out of the Nest

Over the next few months, I became frustrated with the growing pains of a new Christian. I was struggling to overcome decades of bad habits, and guilt over what I had done as Jane Roe still haunted me from time to time.

What kept me going? There's a simple answer: God.

In August 1996 I faced a particularly low point. I spent eleven days in San Diego as O.R. confronted the Republican National Committee, fighting to keep the party on the side of life. This struggle just about removed all signs of life from me!

We sensed the spiritual warfare almost as soon as we arrived. Our schedule was brutal—up at five o'clock, on the streets by six-thirty, and working all day. At night we held rallies, which lasted until ten or eleven, then we grabbed a bite to eat and dropped into bed at midnight or even later.

Since we were sleeping three and four people to a room and since we were all so tired, I gained a more realistic view of the Christian life. Yes, we are changed, but even Christians get tired, short-tempered, and discouraged, and I experienced all three.

Many of the women I worked with served as volunteer sidewalk counselors. They had given up vacation days and sacrificed time with their families to travel to San Diego, at their own expense, for one purpose: to try to convince women not to kill their unborn children.

But when we arrived at the clinics, we found that many of the abortion doctors had decided to close temporarily to avoid protests by Operation Rescue. There were still plenty of people to counsel, however: all the proabortionists who showed up to guard the clinics and women who tried to get into the few clinics that were open. Several of the women changed their minds and chose life for their babies.

This week of confrontation battered my spirit. I had gone to San Diego more than willing to be arrested in defense of life. But each day's battle seemed to take a little piece out of me, and by the end of the eleven days, I could barely stand.

The crisis was this: I knew I was called to love and serve Jesus, and I knew that call included speaking up in defense of life. But was I cut out for the intense confrontations that regularly greeted Operation Rescue volunteers? These were my dearest friends. They had led me to the Lord. But was it possible that God was calling me out of this particular ministry?

When I got back to Dallas, I was exhausted and confused. A still, small voice told me God was calling me to something else, but I did not even want to consider that possibility. I was like a little bird whose mother was trying to push her out of the nest, encouraging her to fly—but I didn't want to fly!

At this moment of near despair, I sat in Hillcrest during a Wednesday evening service and looked up to see a ray of sunlight burst through the windows. Instantly I felt an indescribable peace come over me. I could sense God saying, "You're in a rut, my child. Seek me, for I am Lord."

You're in a rut. It never occurred to me that I could serve God anywhere other than Rescue. In my early days, I would have thought that stepping away from Rescue would be like stepping away from God. But now God was calling me out of my rut—my unexamined thinking—and telling me, "Seek *me,* for I am Lord."

As this new peace overwhelmed me, I was not sure how all this would turn out; but I knew God was behind it. He not only addressed my questions about my future with Rescue, but an even deeper need, which I had ignored: "I have forgiven you, Norma. Now you must take time to forgive yourself."

I realized that I had not completely let go of the guilt I carried for signing that affidavit, and the weight of that guilt was dragging me down. God wanted to lift it.

"Come sit with me, for I am the Lord, and you are my child."

After church I spoke with Pastor Sheats. He listened patiently and urged me to act thoughtfully, not rashly. God would patiently guide me, he said. I could take my time, place my plans in God's hands, and he would direct my paths. I scheduled a meeting with an assistant pastor later in the week, and he reaffirmed Pastor Sheats's encouragement and advice. Though Hillcrest is a relatively large church, the pastors were generous in giving me more than my fair share of time—and there were times I really needed it.

During the following weeks, it became apparent that God was indeed directing me to serve him in a new capacity. To my surprise, I found that Ronda Mackey was also experiencing a change in direction, and she had also sought counsel from Pastor Sheats. Both of us felt God wanted to do a new thing in our lives, and our pastor agreed.

And then, in a tapestry that only God himself could weave, doors began to open for Ronda and me to work together, apart from Operation Rescue. I knew I would always be thankful for the tremendous opportunities I had at Rescue, but it was time to step out in faith to a new calling.

That new calling became known as Roe No More Ministry. Through this ministry, Ronda and I want to be able go out and speak to women, encourage pro-life groups, and do whatever we can to further the cause of life. Ronda is frequently with me on my trips, including a special trip I had to make to Tennessee.

Jane Roe Meets Mary Doe

It was a beautiful Tennessee day on March 23, 1997, when I met Sandra Cano, the woman who signed the other affidavit (as Mary Doe) that brought virtually unregulated abortion to all fifty states. Many people do not realize that *Roe v. Wade* had a very important companion case. While *Roe* struck down the abortion laws of every state in the nation, *Doe v. Bolton,* announced the same day, described a woman's health in such broad terms that even the modest restrictions alluded to in *Roe* were rendered worthless. Doe also said that states could not prohibit abortions performed outside of accredited hospitals, opening the door to the evolution of abortion clinics.

Suddenly, overnight, abortion was legal everywhere, through all nine months of pregnancy, for virtually any reason—thanks to Jane Roe and Mary Doe.

In many ways, Sandra Cano's story is remarkably similar to mine. She dropped out of school in the tenth grade and made a disastrous marital decision at the age of sixteen. Though her husband was in and out of jail on child molestation and kidnapping charges, she managed to conceive and give birth to three children by the time she turned twenty-two.

Following some mental problems, Sandra lost her children: the state placed one for adoption, and two were put in foster care. When she conceived her fourth child, she went to an Atlanta Legal Aid office for help in getting a divorce and getting her children back. There she was put in touch with an American Civil Liberties Union lawyer who told her to sign some papers.

"I'll see what I can do," the attorney said.

The lawyer managed to get the two children in foster care back, and as a favor Sandra allowed the lawyer to use her case to challenge the abortion laws. Sandra never wanted an abortion, she just wanted her children back. In fact, the lawyer arranged for her to get an abortion at an out-of-state hospital, but Sandra refused to go through with it. She later gave birth to a baby girl.

During this period, Sandra had been examined twice at a psychiatric hospital and once admitted to a reporter, "I just had a really tremendous emotional stress on me." Concerning her role in the affidavit, Sandra said she was "like a little puppy on a leash. Wherever I thought anybody was going to help me, I would follow along."

The parallels between our stories are eerie. Both of us dropped out of school, and both of us were very poor. Both of us married abusive men and had our children taken away from us. We even chose the same name for one of our daughters—Melissa. And in 1989, after she started speaking out against her role in *Doe v. Bolton,* Sandra's home, like mine, was targeted in a drive-by shooting.

When Sandra's *Doe* daughter turned nineteen, she held a news conference to announce that she was pro-choice. Guess what lawyer represented her? That's right—Gloria Allred. And, of course, both of our groundbreaking cases were based on lies. I wasn't raped, and Sandra never wanted an abortion.

Though our backgrounds are so similar, in other ways Sandra and I are exact opposites. She is very demure, quiet, and somewhat shy—something I've never been accused of! Sandra's experience with the proabortion movement has not been much different from mine, however.

After hearing the news of my conversion, Sandra wrote a letter to Operation Rescue in which she said, "[*Doe v. Bolton*] is based on fraud, and never should have happened. . . . I never wanted or had an abortion. . . . I was used and manipulated for others. . . . I am pro-life and always have been and always will be. I will never give up the fight to change . . . this terrible law."

Sound familiar?

I had met Sandra before, but today was a special day. We were in Chattanooga to speak out against abortion and to have plaques installed in the National Memorial for Unborn Children. (A transcript of my remarks to the audience is included in the Appendix.)

The memorial plaques, which Sandra and I wrote ourselves, read as follows:

I WAS BORN NORMA MCCORVEY. I BECAME KNOWN AS JANE ROE ON JANUARY 22, 1973, WHEN THE U.S. SUPREME COURT RELEASED THE *ROE V. WADE* DECISION, WHICH CREATED A WOMAN'S RIGHT TO ABORTION.

I WAS BORN SANDRA CANO. I BECAME KNOWN AS MARY DOE ON JANUARY 22, 1973, WHEN THE U.S. SUPREME COURT RELEASED *ROE V. WADE'S* COMPANION DECISION, *DOE V. BOLTON*, WHICH ALLOWED WOMEN TO ABORT FOR ANY REASON.

We are now forgiven and redeemed, new creatures in Christ and children of God.

Today we publicly recant our involvement in the tragedy of Abortion. We humbly ask the forgiveness of the millions of women and unborn babies who experienced the violence of abortion.

In this place of healing, the National Memorial for the Unborn, we stand together to honor the worth of every unborn child as created in the image of God.

March 23, 1997

Norma McCorvey — Sandra Cano

These activities—visiting the Supreme Court, speaking out at rallies, and setting up a plaque at the National Memorial for the Unborn—represent my new calling in life.

God has given me a second chance. Now I want to work so that every child is given the most fundamental chance—the chance to live.

Won by Love

I visit the playground at Hillcrest all the time now. It no longer evokes sad memories of children who never had the chance to live.

Instead, it has become one of my favorite places in all the world—because it's where I hear the laughter of Emily and Chelsey as they jump from swing to slide to the climbing bars. I get to watch their smiles, which reveal those adorable tiny teeth. I get to hear their shrieks of delight, before the world bends their spirits into cynicism. I get to witness the love of life that only a child possesses.

Today it's quiet on the playground. The girls and I are just here on a lunch break. No one else is around, and I think of what God has done for me. I had three chances to be a good mother, and I lost every one of them. I can't go back. Those daughters will never be five years old again. I'll never be able to help them learn to read, or dress them up for church, or have that long talk before their first date.

But I don't feel bitter. God has given me these children, Emily and Chelsey, to enjoy. Emily and Chelsey bear Ronda's last name, but the love that exists between me and them is no less strong because of it. In many ways, I feel as if these girls are mine.

You see, I've found that, in God's world, love has no limits. In the world of abortion, limits determine life. There's not enough love . . . not enough time . . . not enough money . . . not enough housing.

But in God's world, love grows, it doesn't fade. In God's world, time becomes eternal; we prepare our children for a world that will never end. In God's world, bills still need to be paid, but we need never face our obligations without faith. As for housing—God is preparing a mansion for each of us to enjoy.

That's what it's like for me now, in God's world. It's a world where I can get to know one of my natural-born daughters, Melissa, and her children, my granddaughters, Chloe and Jordan. There has been some healing, as well as some rough spots and difficulties; but we're getting there, in God's time, in God's world.

I now have a purpose in life that is bigger than myself. Instead of fighting for death, I'm fighting for life. Instead of drinking beer by the pitcherful, I can't get enough of God's Spirit.

Oh, there are still plenty of problems. I'm nowhere close to perfect. I've been nursing some pretty nasty habits for almost fifty years, so it's going to take some time for all of them to be dealt with. But I'm making headway.

I still struggle with what I call in one poem the "Sea of Bad." In yet another poem, however, one I'd like to share with you, I celebrate the summer of my renewal.

The Summer of My Renewal

My summer of renewal started way back when,
full of drugs and booze and a lot of sin.

I'd hear of people laughing and causing such a stir
that our God was crying, "Oh come out of there.
Reach up and touch me, I'm your truest friend.
Come on, Norma, don't wait until the end."
My summer of renewal started way back when.

My summer of renewal started way back when,
through the bars and honky tonks where I would sin.
Not so pretty in the light of day,
Sadness and anger were just fine.
All I needed was just a little bit of time.
My summer of renewal started way back when.

My summer of renewal started way back when,
in jails, in parks, in alley ways,
where I would lie to mend.
Stay away from cops and kids,
join women on the march
for equal rights and body parts,
found only in a jar.
My summer of renewal started way back when.

The years went by in silent rooms
filled with smoke and screams.
The years went by in silent rooms
filled with empty dreams.

My summer of renewal started way back when,
and I knew I was to blame,
watching empty playgrounds,
hanging my head in shame.
I sobered up and saw what I had done,
destroying innocent children
through the "rights" that I had won.
The summer of my renewal started way back when.

The summer of my renewal started way back when.
The sins we cast are from the past,
Jesus is the way.
You see his smile in every child,
bringing new light to day.
The summer of my renewal started way back when.

I'm not perfect, by any means, but I'm making progress now. I can finally look into the eyes of a man and see love and respect, not hate. I can listen to a child laugh and feel joy, not guilt. I can pass a church and feel peace, not terror.

This is what love has done for my life. This is what happens when Christians are willing to face their enemies and adopt the most powerful strategy ever devised—the strategy displayed by Christ's death on a cross, the strategy of laying down your life so that others, including the unborn, might live.

This is what it is like to be won by love.

Appendix

Transcript of Norma McCorvey's Remarks
National Memorial for Unborn Children
March 23, 1997

Good morning.

The affidavit did not happen the way I said it did, pure and simple. I lied! Sarah Weddington and Linda Coffee needed an extreme case to make their client look pitiable. Rape seemed to be the ticket. What made rape even worse? A gang rape! It all started out as a little lie. I said what I needed to say. But my little lie grew and grew and became more horrible with each telling.

Sarah and Linda's eyes seemed blinded to my obvious inability to tell the same story twice. It was good for the cause! It read well in the newspapers. With the help of a willing *Dallas Morning News* and the credibility of such well-known columnists as Carl Rowan, the lie became the truth these past twenty-five years.

The deceit was exposed in the late '80s with the made-for-TV movie, *Roe v. Wade,* with Holly Hunter. Sarah knew the truth, the real truth, long before she ever went to the Supreme Court in 1971. Yes, the stated reason for my abortion is based upon a lie, a great lie. So the entire abortion industry is based on a lie.

I did not go to several Dallas physicians as the affidavit said I did. In fact I went to one mill, an illegal clinic, that had just been shut down by the police. Back then police arrested abortionists. Today they are arresting gentle Christians laying down their lives to save our Lord's precious children. They are arresting them because of a lie. My lie. I never went to any other place seeking an abortion—except, of course, to Sarah Weddington and Linda Coffee.

I did not come to the Supreme Court on behalf of a class of women. I was not pursuing any legal remedy for my unwanted pregnancy. I did not go to the federal courts for relief. I went to Sarah Weddington asking her if she knew how I could obtain an abortion. She and Linda Coffee said they didn't know where to get one. They lied to me just like I lied to them! Sarah already had an abortion. She knew where to get one. Sarah and Linda were looking for somebody, anybody, to use to further their own agenda. I was their most willing dupe.

For this I will forever be ashamed. But Jesus has saved me from the tentacles of this horrible lie. My life has been restored to me, and I now have the privilege of speaking for those who cannot speak for themselves. My body does not belong to me, it belongs to him who has saved me for his purpose.

Thank you.

Norma McCorvey's Letter to Nelson Mandela, President of South Africa

Dear Mr. Mandela:

Please allow me to introduce myself to you. My name is Norma McCorvey. I'm a forty-nine-year-old woman, a grandmother of two, and now a pro-life activist. It was my test case that opened the floodgates to legalized abortion in the United States. I'm Roe of *Roe v. Wade*.

I feel somehow that you have heard of this tragic case that now faces your nation. When I came out as Jane Roe in 1989, I knew there would be a price to pay, and that payment was made by gunshot blasts coming through my living room windows one morning at about 4 A.M. To this day, I suffer hearing loss in my right ear. I tell you this, sir, to give you some background of my personal testimony. I've worked in abortion clinics here in the States and have at many times been present when women go through abortions.

One day when I was in my office a woman came in and asked for the doctor. When I looked up, I realized she must be six months along, so I told her that she had the wrong office. The OB-GYN clinic was down the hall. Much to my surprise, she said she had an appointment to have an abortion.

I was shocked. I went into the hallway to collect myself and then went back after she had been taken into a procedure room. The woman was smiling and hanging her feet off the table. I leaned over and asked her what caused her to put off the abortion for six months, and she said that she had just found out she was pregnant with a girl and she wanted a boy.

Horrified, I left the room again and cried. I left work early that day and didn't return for two weeks. When I did go back I asked how she was; the doctor told me she was fine and all green lights were in her favor.

One morning she called and said she wanted to see her baby and could we show it to her? I told her that it had been sent to a lab and asked her why would she want to see it anyway. She said she had a dream of the baby the night before and then asked me again for the name of the lab. I wished I could have shown her what she had let the doctor do, but it was too late—too late for her and way too late for the child.

I won't take up more of your time, sir, but I really think that you should reconsider the position you have taken on abortion. You and your wife Winnie fought so hard against apartheid and you sacrificed so much of yourself for your people and your cause. It wouldn't be worth your time or energy to let it all go down the drain now.

I was baptized on August 8th, 1995, in the name of my Lord and Savior Jesus Christ, washed with the blood of the Lamb. I sleep full nights without nightmares, don't drink anymore, and I've been clean and sober for so long that I thank God every morning and every night for dying on that cross on Calvary.

Believe me, sir, your country could possibly have a dark cloud hanging over it, if and when you sign that bill on abortion. I heard a speech in which you said, "Simply say with hope, Good morning." You have such a nice voice that one would think you wouldn't want this horror in your nation. Hasn't there been enough bloodshed?

In closing, please, sir, I beg of you not to do this to your women, your country, and most of all to yourself.

In Jesus' Name,

Miss Norma McCorvey

For more information about Norma McCorvey and Roe No More Ministry, contact her at

Roe No More Ministry
P.O. Box 550626
Dallas, TX 75355-0626
(972) 414-9104

LaVergne, TN USA
11 April 2011
223693LV00001B/22/P

9 780785 286547